MICHAEL FREEMAN
THE PHOTOGRAPHER'S EYE
FIELD GUIDE

The **essential handbook** for traveling with your digital SLR camera

AMSTERDAM • BOSTON • HEIDELBERG • LONDON
NEW YORK • OXFORD • PARIS • SAN DIEGO
SAN FRANCISCO • SINGAPORE • SYDNEY • TOKYO
Focal Press is an imprint of Elsevier

ELSEVIER

**Focal
Press**

Focal Press is an imprint of Elsevier
30 Corporate Drive, Suite 400, Burlington,
MA 01803, USA

This book was conceived, designed,
and produced by Ilex Press Limited
210 High Street, Lewes, BN7 2NS, UK

Publisher: Alastair Campbell
Creative Director: Peter Bridgewater
Managing Editor: Chris Gatcum
Art Director: Julie Weir
Designer: Jon Allan
Art Editor: Emily Harbison

Library of Congress Control Number
A catalog record for this book is available
from the Library of Congress

ISBN: 978-0-240-81248-9

For information on all Focal Press publications visit
our website at: www.focalpress.com

Printed and bound in China

09 10 11 12 12 11 10 9 8 7 6 5 4 3 2 1

CONTENTS

INTRODUCTION

This is what I do for a living. I travel and photograph, for a little more than half of each year. Indeed, my wife calls me a "professional tourist." Actually, I travel to photograph, which is a little different, because each trip has one or more assignments, and there is a distinct, different purpose each time. And for once, I am writing a book partly for my own benefit, a manual that collates the kind of information that I, as a photographer who travels, need.

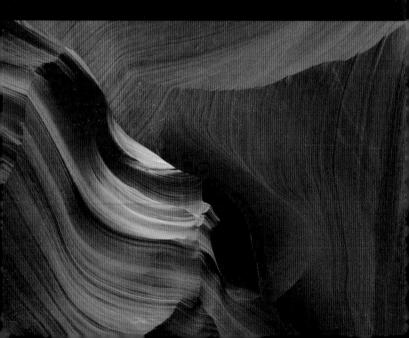

The broad idea of travel has a long and intimate relationship with the camera. By the middle of the nineteenth century photography had become practicable, although by today's standards immensely laborious. The weight of equipment, the difficulty and uncertainty of preparing and processing plates on location did not deter scores of photographers from setting out to explore the world. They had a practical motive for this, because the invention of the new medium coincided with an insatiable demand in the West to know how the world looked—its monuments, landscapes, cultures. Travel photography aimed to satisfy that demand—and has never stopped. The major difference now is that millions of people do it.

Digital photography brings a new element to this. Some may feel a little nervous about taking a digital camera and its paraphernalia on the road. What if it goes wrong? What if the connections are not compatible? Can I find what I need in Bangkok? Or Tulsa? The answers are surprisingly simple, and come down to preparation. The trick is to know what you can plan for and what is best tackled once the trip has started, as you go along. This applies as much to the subjects you are going to photograph as well as to the equipment

you will use. Technically it may be a little more complex than shooting with film, but only because the possibilities are greater for capturing images in all kinds of situations, and for guaranteeing that their qualities of color, contrast, and clarity are as you wanted them to be. If travel broadens the mind, digital cameras broaden travel photography.

JAPANESE GOTHIC

A unique shot of something characterful and spontaneous is always a good idea. This is a shot of a gothic geisha-styled girl in Japan.

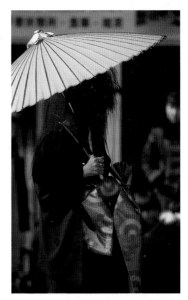

LIGHT AND DARK

One view of the famous slot canyons of Arizona. The play of dark and light makes for a beautiful display of contrast which you should always look out for with your travel photography.

PREPARATION

Before you get out in the field with your camera, it's essential that you spend some time on preparation. The idea here is to make life smooth and easy on the road, so that the adventures are reserved for the place, the people, and your experiences, not the disappointments of missing excellent photo opportunities because you were in the wrong place at the wrong time, your battery packed up, or you ran out of memory cards.

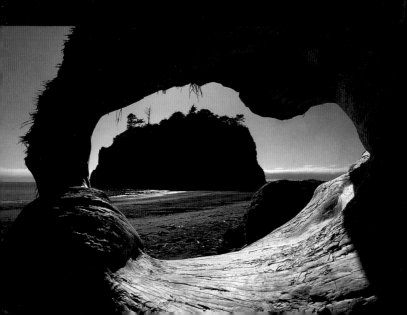

PREPARATION

9

On the road

Appreciating Light

Subject

Themes

Reference

O ver the course of this chapter we'll look at how best to prepare for your trip, whether it's a day's hike in the mountains or an extended travel adventure.

It really pays to find out as much as you can about what you are setting off to photograph, whether it's a place, people, or an event. This doesn't mean that you have to burden yourself with a reference library, but at least cover all the basic information sources, such as guidebooks and anything you can find on the Internet. Researching what you intend, or are likely to want, to photograph will help you assess what equipment you are likely to need and also provide you with the opportunity to read about the experiences of other photographers who have undertaken similar trips. Any helpful hints and tips you can unearth in advance of your travels will help enormously once you're on the road.

There are many ways of traveling with a view to taking photographs. Some travelers like to fix a schedule down to the precise minute, never deviating from their perfect plan. At the opposite extreme are those who steadfastly refuse to commit themselves to anything, determined to follow the whim of the moment. And in between are infinite shades of traveling style. Of course, one of the advantages of planning is that you know in advance exactly which arrangements you absolutely do have to make right now, and which don't matter. If you travel high season anywhere, you have less flexibility than if you are going somewhere unpopular or out of season.

Today, most photographers—whether amateur or professional—who need to travel light when out in the field use digital photography equipment. As so much digital equipment is very specific and cannot be interchanged with that from other manufacturers don't rely on being able to acquire the right bits and pieces on the road. One basic assumption you should make as part of your preparation is that you must have everything that you will need for the camera with you before you leave. It's essential to consider memory cards and spare batteries, plus any other equipment that you can carry easily and which will help get the shots you want, such as filters or additional lenses. Remember to also include any item of equipment that you personally cannot do without.

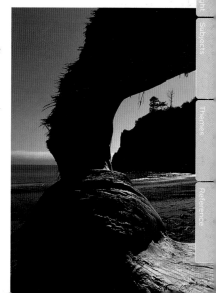

BEING PREPARED

Careful preparation can show you what to expect when you arrive at a location, but it won't tell you everything. In this shot, I knew the rocky island was there, but not the driftwood which forms a perfect frame.

Location, location

Many years ago, while I was being briefed for a book assignment at Time-Life, the Art Director, Lou Klein, gave me a piece of advice in his usual didactic way. "Photography," he said, "is about being in the right place at the right time." Yes, it sounds obvious, but what good advice, because it lays out the priorities. He didn't mention composition, lighting, sense of timing, or any of that, simply because these skills were taken for granted. Of course you had to know how to make a good picture, but the most important thing was to put yourself in the best position to shoot, that advice applies as much to the amateur photographer as it does to the professional.

Maps are the key, whether topographical, street, plans, or even aerial photographs, all of which are available in surprising abundance for most destinations. Having a map makes everything quicker and avoids wasting time and getting lost. I rely heavily on them, whether it's a street map for city shooting or a topographical map for trekking and landscapes. If you're keen on landscapes, for example, a topographical map will not only show you where you're likely to capture a good view (it may even show you recognized "viewpoints"), but you'll also be able to work out from the map the direction in which the sun will rise and set—essential if you want to be in position and prepared in advance for either one or other solar event.

Equally, a street map used in conjunction with a good city guidebook will help you to find the sights you want to photograph so that you can plan your route efficiently. You'll also be able to assess how close you are to other sights and sounds of the city that might have greater appeal to any non-photographers on the trip!

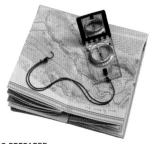

BEING PREPARED
Taking a map and compass with you on your walking trips will save you lots of confusion.

Postcards

For a quick preview of the local sights, take a look at the postcard rack at the airport or hotel lobby. Even though you may not be tempted to shoot a similar view, the local photographers know what is where.

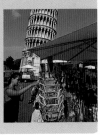

There are many different series of guidebooks, and the value of all these is principally in their coverage of practicalities, including internal travel, hotels, and restaurants. For a visual briefing look to illustrated books and back-issues of magazines such as National Geographic and GEO, as these will give you a better idea of the local photo opportunities.

PREPARATION

11

On the road

Appreciating Light

Subjects

Themes

Reference

USING MAPS
It is always a good idea to have a map and compass handy wherever you plan to walk. It can be a lifesaver if you are trekking somewhere you haven't been before.

WALKING MAPS AND BOOKS
When researching locations, find as much information as you can in guidebooks and walking maps.

Global Positioning System

Now that GPS receivers are small and accurate, they are becoming part of the standard equipment for serious travelers.

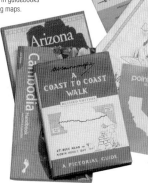

Setting your own goals

Although a professional photographer is under constant pressure to deliver good pictures, one distinct benefit is that professional photography is always focused—there is an aim, which usually begins with a brief from a client. As a keen amateur or aspiring professional it's possible to replicate this focus by assigning yourself certain goals. Self-assignment is not just as an exercise, but an important outlet for your imagination and a way of directing your efforts. The aim might be to show a certain aspect of a location, an event, a ceremony, an activity, a cultural feature—the possibilities are endless. Nevertheless, it is important to set this out in advance, because this in turn has to be fleshed out into a shotlist.

A shotlist is self-defining, but usually begins with jotted notes from your research into the place you plan to visit. In practice, shotlists are dynamic rather than static. They get added to and subtracted from as you continue to photograph. You can follow a shotlist methodically or use it simply as an occasional reminder, depending on how you like to work and the type of vacation or traveling you've embarked on. Certain images that seem a good idea in advance may turn out to be impractical, unachievable, or simply not so strong after all. Other possibilities will suggest themselves on the spot.

ROOM WITH A VIEW
Always keep an eye open for unusual viewpoints. This was one of several shots I took at the Lake Palace hotel, occupying its own island in the middle of Lake Pichola, Udaipur, one of the most picturesque cities of Rajasthan.

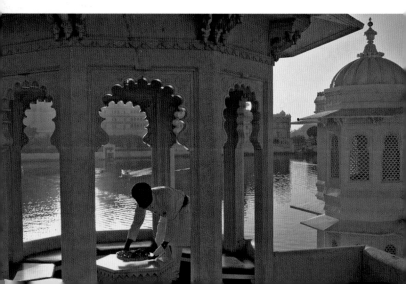

PREPARATION

13

On the road

Appreciating Light

Subjects

Themes

Reference

There is then the matter of treatment and style. Thinking about these at the start can help add depth to your photography and inject originality. There are some low-level practical considerations, such as the following:

- Which focal lengths of lens to concentrate on, for the character they give.
- What natural lighting conditions to look for.
- Shooting at different scales, from distant to close (long views to close-up details).
- Whether to stress the continuity of images or variety.

The higher-level aspects of treatment and style are more difficult to pin down, being dependent on a photographer's ability and creativity. Nevertheless, it helps to develop and follow your own way of choosing, composing, and lighting images.

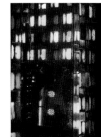

FAIRY LIGHTS
This night-time view of Lake Palace hotel was shot using a tripod and a long exposure to make the most of the beautiful lighting.

ON THE WATERFRONT
A different viewpoint of Lake Palace hotel from the waters of Lake Pichola.

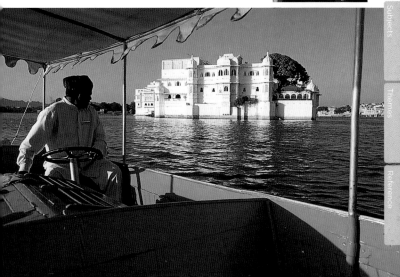

Camera choices

There are three basic types of digital camera available today, all of which are suitable for photography in the field (I exclude backs for medium- and large-format cameras). They are:

○ Compacts
○ Fixed-lens (prosumer) SLR-like models
○ Digital SLRs

Each has its advantages and disadvantages, and the right equipment depends ultimately on the use you intend to make of the finished images.

Although there are now some compact cameras that boast a resolution of 14+ megapixels—comparable to many digital SLRs—because of their relatively small sensors when compared with a digital SLR, image quality, particularly in low light and/or with a high ISO setting, is unlikely to be sufficiently good enough for general print publication. So if you're hoping to sell your images to a stock agency a compact camera is unlikely to provide you with acceptable results. However, for a web blog, for example, or as a personal record for friends and family, most compact cameras are capable of producing perfectly acceptable results.

Fixed-lens prosumer models are, in relation to digital SLRs, light and compact, considerable advantages for traveling. The better models, particularly those with larger-sized sensors, can produce excellent images which wouldn't look out of place in a magazine or book. However, a prosumer camera won't produce consistently high-quality images that would satisfy a picture agency.

Digital SLRs (DSLRs) tend to be more rugged, accept a wide range of lenses, and, particularly those that feature full-frame (35mm) sensors, will provide superb image quality. If your intention is to get your images published as widely as possible, then a DSLR (with a selection of good quality lenses) is your best option. Weight is, nevertheless, an important consideration when traveling, so think about what you're going to do with your images and weigh up the pros and cons of each camera type.

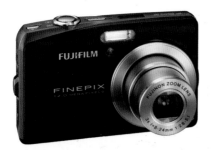

COMPACT CAMERA
Many modern compact cameras boast high resolution figures, in excess of 10 megapixels.

PREPARATION

15

On the road

Appreciating Light

Subjects

Themes

Reference

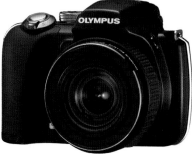

SUPERZOOM CAMERA
Fixed-lens, prosumer "superzoom" cameras combine high-resolution sensors with zoom lenses that go from wide-angle to ultra-telephoto, so there's no need to carry around a heavy bag full of lenses.

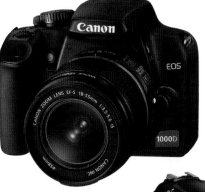

ENTRY LEVEL DSLR
An "entry-level" digital SLR will typically feature an APS-C-sized sensor (22 x 15 mm) with a resolution of between 10 and 15 megapixels, and is capable of producing excellent results, even in low light.

PROFESSIONAL DSLR
An increasing number of pro-spec digital SLRs feature a full-frame (35 mm) sensor and a resolution of over 20 megapixels. The image quality of such cameras is comparable to that of a medium-format film camera.

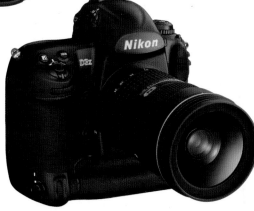

DSLR travel kit

Weighing 26lb (12kg), this is no lightweight configuration, and was assembled specifically for a serious hike in the hills. If the trek involves overnight camping for two or three days, the number of spare batteries and memory cards will have to be worked out very carefully from your own experience of how you shoot.

Needless to say, halfway up Helvellyn or on a trans-Himalayan pass is not the place to run out of either of these. Although specfically a trekking backback, by dispensing with a few items, such as the walking pole, water bottle, guides, maps, and knife, you have a DSLR kit that would cover pretty much most photographic opportunities.

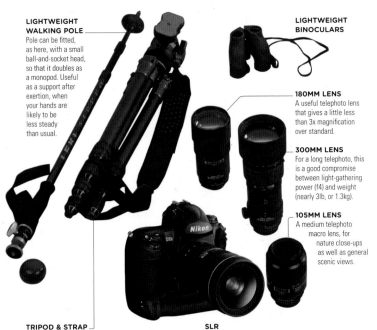

LIGHTWEIGHT WALKING POLE
Pole can be fitted, as here, with a small ball-and-socket head, so that it doubles as a monopod. Useful as a support after exertion, when your hands are likely to be less steady than usual.

LIGHTWEIGHT BINOCULARS

180MM LENS
A useful telephoto lens that gives a little less than 3x magnification over standard.

300MM LENS
For a long telephoto, this is a good compromise between light-gathering power (f4) and weight (nearly 3lb, or 1.3kg).

105MM LENS
A medium telephoto macro lens, for nature close-ups as well as general scenic views.

TRIPOD & STRAP
Extra weight, but important if you intend to shoot at speeds slower than 1/30 sec. This model is light, but expensive—carbon fiber with a magnesium alloy ball head, weighing 3.5lb (1.6kg).

SLR
Your SLR camera will determine which lenses and accessories you can use.

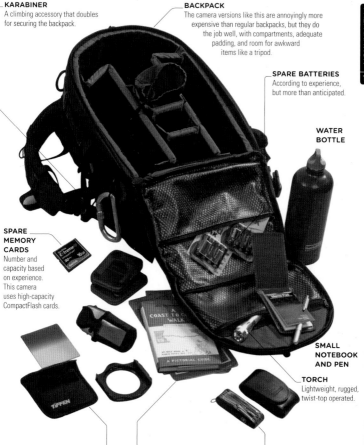

KARABINER
A climbing accessory that doubles for securing the backpack.

BACKPACK
The camera versions like this are annoyingly more expensive than regular backpacks, but they do the job well, with compartments, adequate padding, and room for awkward items like a tripod.

SPARE BATTERIES
According to experience, but more than anticipated.

WATER BOTTLE

SPARE MEMORY CARDS
Number and capacity based on experience. This camera uses high-capacity CompactFlash cards.

SMALL NOTEBOOK AND PEN

TORCH
Lightweight, rugged, twist-top operated.

FILTER HOLDER AND GRAD
Neutral grad filter for darkening skies, needs a holder which allows it to be moved up and down, and rotated. Adaptor rings for fitting to various lens diameters.

WAINWRIGHT AND MAP
Trekking guide and map. In this case, for a walk across England from the Lake District, the famous hand-drawn, hand-written Wainwright Coast to Coast.

SWISS ARMY KNIFE
All-in-one emergency small tool.

Camera accessories

One accessory that you should seriously consider taking with you when in the field is a tripod. Most photographers have mixed feelings about tripods. On the one hand they are undeniably useful in adding to the range of images you can get on a trip, such as night-time views, as well as enabling you to obtain sharp images even at slow shutter speeds. On the other hand, they weigh extra, are not much fun, and slow down the pace of shooting. How much more pleasant and looser to simply walk and shoot hand-held.

Travel for even a few days, however, increases the chance that you may need a tripod, and most photographers planning a long trip will at least take a tripod along, even if it stays in the vehicle or hotel room for most of the time. Make sure you choose a model that can comfortably support your camera with the zoom set to its longest focal length (or with the longest lens you have if using a DSLR). Cost enters the equation for travel, because strong, light materials are available and they are always more expensive.

Finally, there are good impromptu alternatives to tripods, depending on how slow a shutter speed you need. To hold the camera more steadily, a rolled-up cloth or soft camera bag on a solid surface (such as a wall) works very well—if you press down on the camera or lens as you shoot, you may be able to use shutter speeds as slow as one second.

There's a huge array of other camera accessories available today, some of which are shown on these pages. It's very tempting to talk yourself into thinking that you'll need everything you can possibly imagine when on the road, but do bear in mind that you may end up carrying your equipment for

long periods of time over lengthy distances so only take those accessories that are essential for your photography.

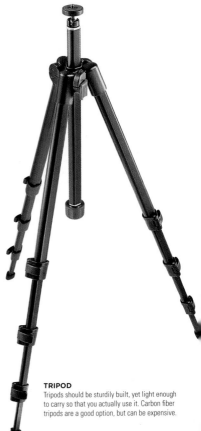

TRIPOD
Tripods should be sturdily built, yet light enough to carry so that you actually use it. Carbon fiber tripods are a good option, but can be expensive.

PREPARATION

19

On the road

Appreciating Light

Subjects

Themes

Reference

Monopod

A single adjustable pole can improve the shutter speed at which you shoot by about a factor of two, and there are numerous monopods available for just this purpose. If you are trekking, look for a walking pole that is fitted with a ⅜ in (9 mm) screw that will accept a small tripod head: two items in one cuts down on your packing and the weight you're carrying.

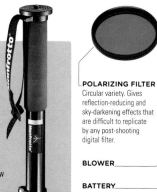

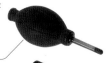

UV FILTER
Colorless. Serves the double function of reducing UV and protecting the delicate front surface of the lens.

POLARIZING FILTER
Circular variety. Gives reflection-reducing and sky-darkening effects that are difficult to replicate by any post-shooting digital filter.

BLOWER

BATTERY

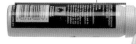

COMPRESSED AIR
Not for the sensor, but for the outside of equipment.

Mini-tripod

Surprisingly useful, being light enough to carry without noticing. What it lacks is elevation, but there are often surfaces to give height, such as a vehicle roof. One good technique is to press the mini-tripod against a vertical surface, such as a wall.

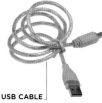

USB CABLE

CARD READER

Protecting your camera

There are three extreme environmental conditions that could adversely affect your camera's operation—cold, heat and dust, and water. Let's take a look at each one in turn. The operating conditions for most digital cameras and media is 32°F to 104°F (0°C to 40°C). Below freezing, there is an increasing risk of failure, and in intense cold (-68°F/-20°C and below), metal, and some plastics can become more brittle and subject to cracking if knocked hard. More immediately obvious is that metal will stick to the skin—very painful to remove—so use gloves when handling and exercise caution when holding close to your cheek and nose. In any case, expose the camera to the full cold only when shooting. For the rest of the time keep it well wrapped in a padded waterproof bag or else carry it on a strap against your chest underneath a front-zippered parka.

Batteries deliver less power at low temperatures and will need to be replaced more frequently. Allow for this in the number of batteries you carry, and prepare to recharge more frequently than usual. Carry spare batteries in a warm place, such as your pants' pocket.

Extreme heat can also cause failure in the camera, media, and batteries. Very high temperatures are less noticeable in dry air as the body feels less discomfort than when conditions are humid, so monitor the equipment particularly carefully in arid, desert locations, and do not expose cameras to direct sun. As with cold weather, it is always best to keep the camera in a bag until you need to shoot.

The second great problem with dry heat is dust, sand, and grit, more common than in humid conditions and more likely to be airborne. Particles can penetrate joints and will cause abrasive damage to moving parts (even though there are fewer mechanical movements in a digital camera than in a traditional film model), and are very difficult to remove. A special problem for digital cameras is the danger of particles settling on the sensor, which will cause artifacts on every shot. Try to avoid changing lenses in such conditions, but if you must, try to find a sheltered place in which to do so, and expose the camera to the air only when shooting. In obviously dusty conditions, such as a duststorm or in a vehicle being driven on an unpaved road, place everything in a large plastic bag and tie it up.

Finally, water in all its forms, from condensation to a complete dunking, is particularly damaging to cameras and lenses. A few drops of rain are harmless, but the amount of water penetration depends on the build quality of the camera. The priority is to keep cameras dry, which means at least under cover in wet conditions. If you know in advance that this will be difficult, investigate whether a waterproof housing is available for your particular camera. Depending on the design of the camera, it might also be possible to rig up impromptu waterproofing with a clear plastic bag and rubber bands.

By the sea, saltwater and salt spray (the latter common in windy weather) bring the added risk of corrosion. Wipe the camera frequently with a clean, dry cloth, and at the end of the day go over all surfaces again, using a damp cloth first. If you drop a camera in water, retrieve it immediately, shake it, open everything that can be opened, wipe off what water you can, then use a blowdryer gently to dry the inaccessible areas.

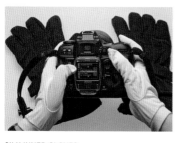

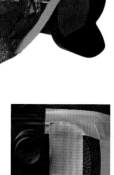

SPACE BLANKET
Light and compact, a space
blanket in metalized polyester
is ideal for wrapping equipment.
Also useful for people.

SILK INNER GLOVES
One solution when handling extremely cold equipment is to
wear silk inner gloves, which are efficient for short periods
when the outer pair is removed.

ZIPLOCK PLASTIC BAGS
Keeps things dry and good
for organizing small,
loose objects.

REFLECTIVE FOIL
As a rule, you should never leave
equipment exposed to direct sunlight
in hot conditions. If, for any reason,
this is unavoidable, keep it covered
with something highly reflective,
such as foil or a space blanket.

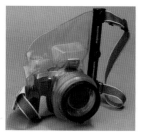

FLEXIBLE CASE
This sealed plastic container is
flexible enough to allow use of
the camera, with a special clear
lenspiece, but sturdy enough to
make it waterproof.

TAPE OVER THE CRACKS
One part of a digital camera
that is always susceptible to dust
and sand is the memory card
compartment. Consider using duct
tape or insulating tape to seal this.

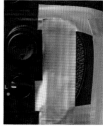

ON THE ROAD

Once your trip is under way, the rules and the skillsets change. Adaptation, response, and improvization combine to make up the new order. Unfortunately, all too typically these are first brought into play because of something left behind. Experienced travelers know better than to expect total efficiency in their own preparation, and instead allow for a logistical gap in the packing list.

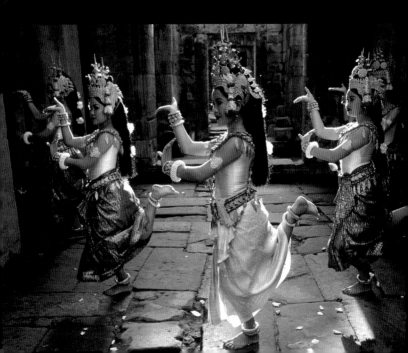

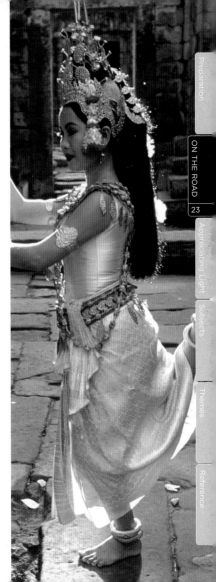

Although leaving something behind
at home as fundamental as a battery
charger may well seem disastrous on the
day of arrival at your destination, in
practice few things are irreplaceable.
Enter the world of the workaround. There
is a cut-off point to preparation, before
which everything is possible, but after
which travel has to be dealt with on an
ad hoc basis, and preferably in that frame
of mind. Being on the road is a kind of
liberation, as in the book of the same title
by Jack Kerouac, and it calls for a shift in
emphasis from careful planning to on-the-
spot reaction. Which ultimately means
encountering and enjoying the unexpected.

TRAVEL PHOTOGRAPHY AND SPONTANEITY

Travel photography is concerned with how things actually
are, with a strong dose of documentary. But quite often
events are openly staged for people's enjoyment, and the
photographer's usual problem is finding a vantage point for
effective shots when there is an audience that also wants
a good view of what is happening.

Preparation

ON THE ROAD

23

Appreciating Light

Subjects

Themes

Reference

Forecasting weather

Weather is the immediate, day-to-day expression of climate. Assuming you have been able to choose the right season for shooting in your destination, you will still usually need to check the weather. How important this is depends on the kind of climate you are in—in some, such as Mediterranean or Savannah, certain times of the year may be completely reliable, day after day. In others, such as the Marine climate of Western Europe, much less so. In addition, the reliability of weather reports varies—Western Europe is particularly difficult for prediction because of the string of complex weather systems approaching it from the Atlantic.

The sources for weather information are:

○ Online. There are both International and national weather websites, and these include the following:

   Weather Channel
   http://www.weather.com/
   Weather Underground
   http://www.wunderground.com/
   National Weather Service [US]
   http://www.nws.noaa.gov/
   Accu Weather
   http://www.accuweather.com/

○ Local radio and television stations.

○ Telephone weather services, some of them specific to cellphone networks.

For photography, the most important weather information is usually the forecast for sunshine, clouds, and rain. All three are related, as clouds are condensed water vapor in moist air. Most of the world's rainfall occurs when two different air masses meet. The line where they meet is called a front, and the warm air tends to rise above the cold, making rain likely. Western Europe and the northwest United States receive most of their weather this way, with a succession of fronts moving eastward. This accounts for the sequence of clouds, rain, and clear skies, and the timing is difficult to predict.

There are two other common kinds of rainfall. One is convectional, and occurs in many parts of the tropics and on hot days in landlocked plains. As the ground heats up during the day, the lower air also heats, and rises rapidly. As it rises, it cools, and loses its ability to hold water vapor, and the result can be vertical stormclouds several miles high, with dramatic anvil-shaped thunderheads and violent rain accompanied by thunder and lightning. The other is orographic, and this occurs when moving air meets mountains and hills. They force the airflow to rise, and if it is already moist, it cools and can no longer hold the water vapor, which condenses quickly.

Clouds as light vs. subject

Cloud cover impacts on photography in its effect on lighting—it blocks the sun to varying degrees acccording to how dense the clouds are. But it can also feature in images as a key element. Distinctly shaped clouds tend to make the most interesting picture elements, and these include fair-weather cumulus, high wispy cirrus, and the anvil-shaped cumulo-nimbus of convectional thunderstorms. Clouds also respond to sunlight in endless ways.

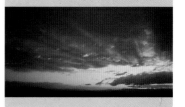

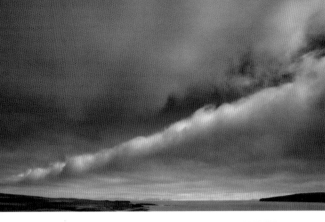

Preparation

ON THE ROAD

25

Appreciating Light

Subjects

Themes

Reference

RECOGNIZE THE SIGNS
It helps to become familiar with local sky patterns and conditions—and to understand what they mean. This advancing line of clouds at a low altitude over Scotland clearly suggests a demarcation between types of air— and is part of a cold front, making showers likely.

DRAMATIC WEATHER
Because of the impossibility of predicting lightning strikes, the best thing is to leave the shutter open until a strike occurs. This means shooting when it is fairly dark to avoid overexposing the scene.

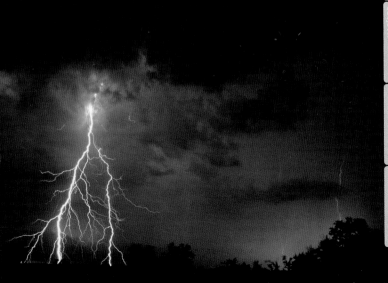

Varying your shots

Travel photography is inevitably about a sense of place, and this has many different expressions. In any one location you can expect to find all kinds of views, incidents, and imagery—provided that you make a conscious effort to vary the way you shoot. Think of the collection of images that accumulates over a day's shooting as a set to be viewed together. They will acquire more combined impact if they have variety in appearance.

Checklist

- Frame vertical as well as horizontal where appropriate.
- Try a range of scales.
- Keep on the lookout for close-ups.
- Where possible include a wide, establishing view, or even a panorama.
- Vary focal length for character as well as convenience.
- Look for graphic, even abstract compositions, as well as the more predictable.

The value of focal length

Shooting with a variety of focal lengths brings diversity to the shoot, not so much because they allow you to cover more or less of a scene from one viewpoint than because they have their own graphic identities. Wide-angle lenses (and the wide end of a zoom range) naturally cover more of a scene than usual, but they have other, subtle qualities. By compressing a wide angle of view, they create a strong perspective that can give photographs a distinctive flavor. Lines and shapes are stretched toward the edges—and even more toward the corners—giving an exaggerated perspective. Diagonals become a strong part of wide-angle views, often converging toward the distance. You can use these to put energy into a photograph, but beware of distortion that simply looks odd—as a rule, avoid placing obvious shapes like circles or faces near the corners. With telephotos, too, there is more to the kind of image than just the coverage. Long focal lengths give a compressed perspective, which can make interesting compositions in which the planes of a scene are "stacked" one behind the other, and makes distant objects seem much larger. Telephotos are good for isolating and emphasizing a single subject. Their depth of field is very shallow, which helps subjects stand out against blurred backgrounds.

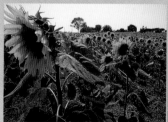 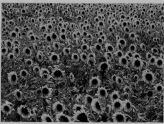

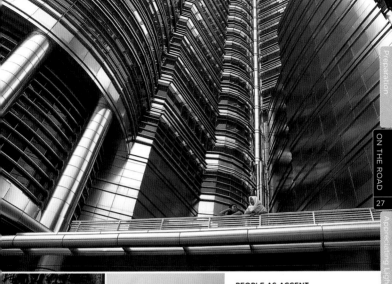

Preparation

ON THE ROAD

27

Appreciating Light

Subjects

Themes

Reference

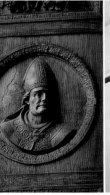

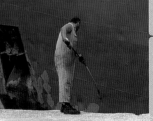

PEOPLE AS ACCENT
Two women against the Petronas Towers, Kuala Lumpur. Shooting with a wide-angle lens makes the most of a strong contrast between people and environment.

DETAIL
The carved wooden door of an Italian church. Closing in on details extends the range of experience.

ABSTRACTION
Fog over San Francisco's Golden Gate Bridge gave an opportunity to create an abstract pattern from a detail of the structure, using a long (400mm efl) lens.

ISOLATING COLOR
The attraction here was less the work going on than the classic color combination of orange and blue. Closing in on the scene to avoid the surroundings made the most of this.

Planning for special events

Parades, processions, fairs, and other public events offer some of the richest and most colorful possibilities for photography. There is never any shortage of scenes and people, and usually the only real difficulty is working your way around the crowds. Because of the high concentration of activity, the key to shooting comprehensively is planning. This means working things out well beforehand, and following a schedule, such as the following:

- ○ The first step is finding out what events are on the calendar for the period you will be at your destination. Before you travel, check in guidebooks, and with the local, regional, or national tourist organization (website or telephone). If the event is well-known, such as Mardi Gras, look for previous photography in magazines such as National Geographic.
- ○ Most events are organized, at least to some extent. If possible, find out what happens when from the organizers, or the local newspaper, local guides, or your hotel.
- ○ Once you know the structure and timing of the event, you can decide which aspects of it are worth photographing, and whether you will have enough time to move from one place to another (in the case of a parade).

- ○ Finding the right viewpoint is essential. In fact, for the key shot (there nearly always is one for most events), viewpoint is everything. Look around the site or the route to find the best vantage points.
- ○ Somewhere high, like a balcony, is often a good bet, allowing you a variety of images with different lenses or zoom settings.
- ○ One of the best ground-level views of a parade is head-on with a telephoto lens. A bend in the road or a traffic island are likely to be good positions for an unobstructed shot.

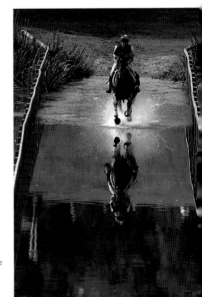

BLENHEIM CROSS-COUNTRY
The cross-country event, featuring a water crossing and brush jump, at horse trials at Blenheim Palace, England. A position high on the opposite bank, recce'd earlier, gave a clearer view with a long telephoto (300mm efl) than from a viewpoint closer to the jump. Head-on shooting also made it easier to get a sequence of frames.

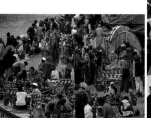

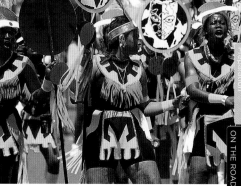

FIRE CEREMONY ON THE GANGES

Each sunset at the holy town of Haridwar on the Ganges in northern India, a Hindu ceremony is performed by priests swinging braziers. The event is always crowded, but a little research earlier in the day identified an area on the opposite bank as ideal for an unobstructed telephoto view. To get a water's-edge position meant arriving an hour before.

KINGSTON CARNIVAL

The annual Carnival in the Jamaican capital is full of color and energy, best captured from the middle of the event. A talk with organizers established permission and also that there would be gaps between groups of dancers from where I could shoot toward the front of each.

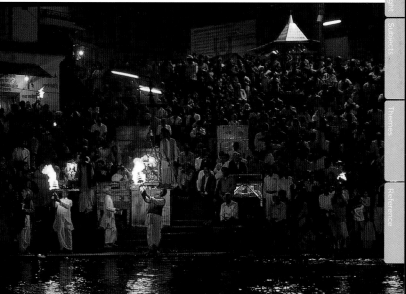

Photographing special events

Events offer several different kinds of image opportunity, and it's important to keep all of these in mind. Most turn on one or two key moments, such as the high point of a procession, so always try and make sure you get these. Nevertheless, don't ignore the other possibilities, which include the asides, the unpredictable events, and behind-the-scenes preparations. To cover as much as possible, you may need to make sure that you can move around, which may not be easy in heavy crowds.

Preparations in the lead up to an event, which may take a few hours, even days, always provide many good opportunities. During these times, which include rehearsals, the pressure is usually off, participants are less keyed-up, and you will usually have much better access than during the event itself. Immediately prior to a parade, participants will gather in one or more staging areas, and these too offer a particular kind of image.

Parades vary in style and organization from place to place, but there are usually some consistent features that lend themselves to these kinds of shot:

○ Long-shot from head-on. Usually, this only works with the head of the parade or if there are distinct breaks between sections.

○ Long-shot from above, cropped in and compressed, showing a mass of people.

○ Wide-angle from close, taking in the energy and the crowd reaction.

○ Close shot of the main character/ float/ centerpiece. You may need to react quickly and choose the right focal length.

○ Spectator reaction. Turn to look at the spectators. Their reactions can make good images in themselves.

○ Details. Look for close-ups, even extreme, of costumes, uniforms, decorations, and so on. Some of these may be quite special and only brought out for this occasion.

Memory management

Events encourage heavy shooting, and with digital there are no concerns about wasting shots. The chief problem is having sufficient memory for the occasion. At the least, clear all your memory cards. In pauses during the day, when not much is happening, you could edit the images.

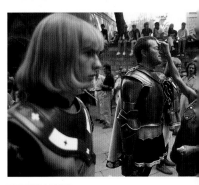

THE SIENA PALIO
This violent and idiosyncratic horse-race takes place annually in the Tuscan city of Palio, dates back to the Middle Ages, and has not changed substantially in all that time. These four images are a small selection of the entire take, chosen here to illustrate variety and coverage.

PREPARATION
Pageant participants (above) being checked for costume and makeup.

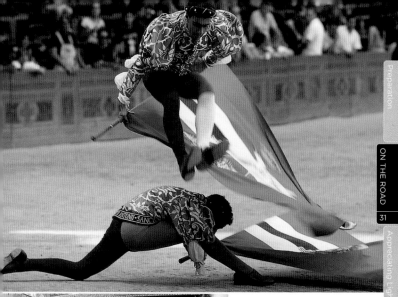

Preparation

ON THE ROAD

31

Appreciating Light

Subjects

Themes

Reference

ACROBATICS
A long pageant precedes the race proper.

THE RACE
No saddles and hardly any rules as the horses complete several circuits of the track in the main piazza.

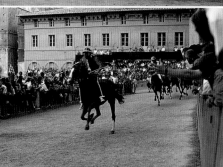

THE CROWD
As well as the event itself, turning your camera on the crowd can reward you with some spontaneous reaction shots.

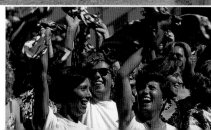

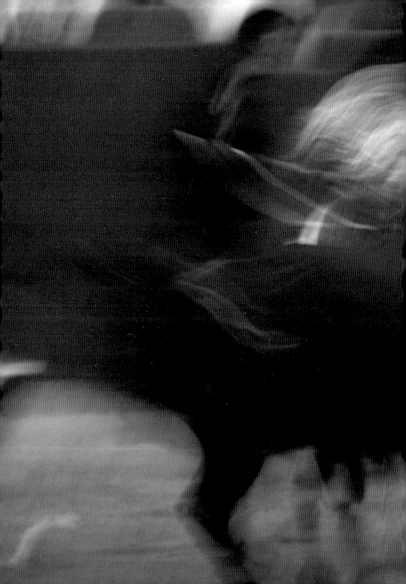

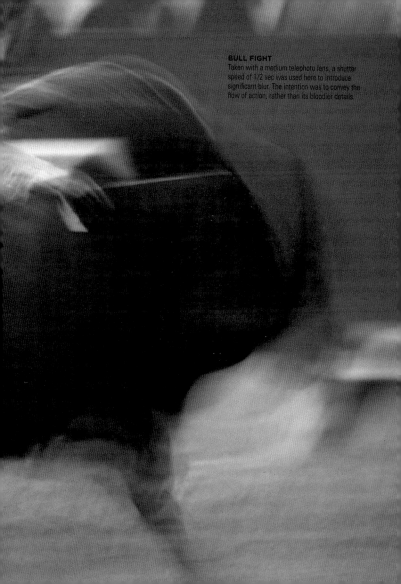

BULL FIGHT
Taken with a medium telephoto lens, a shutter speed of 1/2 sec was used here to introduce significant blur. The intention was to convey the flow of action, rather than its bloodier details.

Photographing an arranged event

Events always need to be organized by someone, so if you're taking your travel photography really seriously, with a view to selling images to an agency or a specific publication, why not arrange your own?

Now, organizing a situation for photography smacks of interference in the normal course of activity, with overtones of pretence. There is, however, the world of a difference between a setup that pretends to be real when it isn't, and a performance that is simply dedicated to one camera. Travel photography is for the most part concerned with how things actually are, with a strong dose of documentary, and the idea of an out-and-out setup is anathema—where a photographer is trying to fool the audience into believing that here is a genuine, spontaneous slice of life when, in reality, the action has been stage-managed. But quite often, as we've seen, events are openly staged for people's enjoyment, and the photographer's usual problem is finding a vantage point for effective shots when there is an audience that also wants a good view of what is happening.

In this case, the performance in question was a traditional Khmer dance staged in the ruins of a 12th-century temple at Angkor, Cambodia. Specifically, and what made it interesting, the gallery where the dances occasionally took place was originally built for that, with stone friezes high up on the walls showing the medieval dancers. The events were arranged by the World Monuments Fund, responsible for the restoration of this particular Angkorean temple. I knew what I wanted—a scene as close to the original as possible. That meant no tourists in view and a certain amount of theatrical direction. It also meant hiring the troupe myself. To get

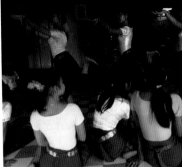

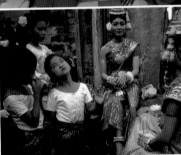

TRADITIONAL DANCE
These images are selected from a shoot at a 12th-century temple at Angkor, and at the dance school where the participants trained.

other shots, I visited the dance school in town and photographed rehearsals there. On the day, I knew from experience that makeup and other behind-the-scenes activities were likely to provide some spontaneous moments.

Preparation

ON THE ROAD

35

Appreciating Light

Subjects

Themes

Reference

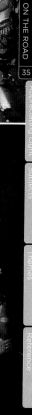

Dealing with obstructions

Popular sights attract people and are often under repair—it can be frustrating to find that the monument you planned to shoot is under scaffolding. Time was when you would have to resign yourself to the loss of a picture. Digital imaging, however, provides the means to restore a scene, and most people are already familiar with the cloning and retouching tools in image-editing software. Here is not the place for detailed instruction in image retouching—the important thing when photographing an obstructed view is to know what can be done digitally and how to shoot for it.

Think of obstructions in terms of their removability, which varies. If the obstruction is at some distance from your subject, it may be possible to move right up to it and shoot wide-angle. Alternatively, a power line that hangs right in front of you from your first choice of viewpoint may, from a distance, reduce to insignificance or be hidden by something innocuous like trees.

When you've done your best on the ground, it's time to plan for the digital retouching. In nearly all cases, removing obstructions digitally means cloning from elsewhere in the image, so these clone sources are the parts to think about. A patterned surface, such as brickwork, is relatively easy to use, but check carefully what the obstruction is covering. If it is hiding a unique feature, such as the doorway of a building, then consider moving the camera slightly. The principle is to choose the viewpoint so that, as far as possible, only clonable areas are hidden.

Even more effective is the parallax system for retouching. For this to work, there has to be some distance between obstruction and subject, so that shifting the viewpoint to one side actually has a parallax effect, revealing unobstructed parts. Scaffolding built close to a building responds poorly to this technique. The ideal result is a pair of near-identical images, but with the parts that are obscured in the first shot revealed in the second. The digital technique is then straightforward; it consists of placing one image in a layer over another and erasing selectively.

1. A CONSTANT CROWD
This Roman monument at Ephesus, Turkey, was immensely popular. I spent ten minutes shooting the identical framing several times.

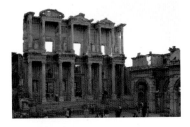

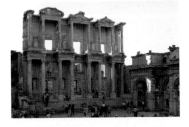

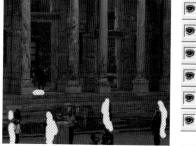

👁	🖌	🖼	Layer 5
👁		🖼	Layer 4
👁		🖼	Layer3
👁		🖼	Layer 2
👁		🖼	Layer 1
👁		🖼	*Background* 🔒

2. LAYERED REMOVAL
Placing each image in a stack, the people were removed with an eraser brush. Because they were moving, what was obscured in one layer was visible in another.

3. FLATTENED COMPOSITE
The holes in each layer created by people removal were automatically filled by the revealed parts of the monument in another layer, and the final composite shows an emptied site.

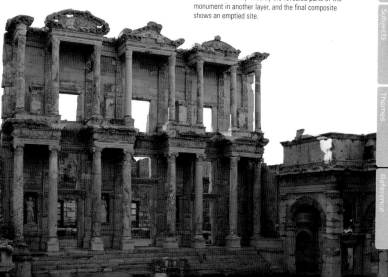

Forward digital planning

The digital solutions to obstructed views on the previous pages are just one example of an essential difference between digital and traditional film cameras: with digital the photography does not end with the capture of the image. The final image is whatever you decide it should be. Post-production is the term used for the work performed on images after shooting to turn them into their final form. Think of it as an extension to shooting.

Indeed, taking full advantage of the freedom and flexibility offered by digital capture calls for a different approach to photography itself. And, as with traveling and travel photography, the principle is forward planning: shooting now with a view to what can be done later. I'm not suggesting that alteration and manipulation should be standard, but there are already several established possibilities, with new ones waiting to be discovered. The established routes include digital removal of unwanted objects, as we've just seen, and also conversion to black-and-white and panoramas, both of which are dealt with on the next pages.

Other possibilities suggest themselves. For example, photographing the identical scene under different lighting conditions provides interesting material for subtle digital manipulation. With just a pair of shot versions, sunlit and cloudy, you can create any combination of the two. Superimpose one over the other in perfect register, as two layers in an image-editing program, and use a paintbrush or eraser to create the effect of a burst of sunlight illuminating just a part of the subject.

The same technique is useful for handling a high range of brightness, such as on a bright cloudy day when a correctly exposed landscape leaves the sky washed out and white. In this case a second exposure, a few stops darker, to record sky detail, can later be combined with the first shot.

1. MANAGING DIFFICULT CONTRAST

Part of digital shooting is knowing what can be done later—and preparing for that work. Here, the juxtaposition of a huge religious monument and tilting power cables in Japan was appealing, but the weather and lighting were unhelpful. But I knew that this could be dealt with provided that I shot in Raw format and avoided overexposure.

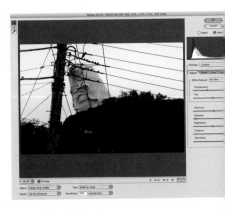

Preparation

ON THE ROAD

39

Appreciating Light

Subjects

Themes

Reference

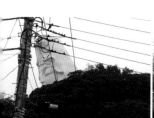

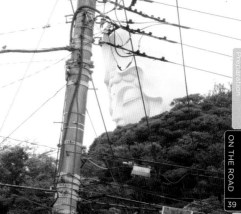

2. RAW BRIGHTS
The Raw image was processed a first time to keep detail in the highlights.

3. RAW DARKS
The same Raw image was processed again, this time to keep detail in the shadow areas. The shadow image was then pasted onto the highlight image in a new layer.

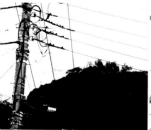

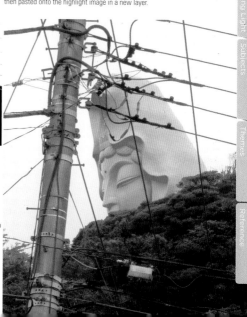

4. L.A.B LEVELS
The light version was then converted to Lab mode, the Lightness channel given extreme contrast by adjusting Levels, and this turned into a selection—in effect a highlight mask.

5. COMPOSITE
After loading the highlight-mask selection into the upper, brighter layer, the Delete button was hit, creating a composite that preserves all the important tones and colors.

Switching to black and white

Most digital cameras offer the option of shooting in monochrome, and although most camera owners ignore this setting, it has exciting possibilities. Black-and-white photography is by no means a reduced version of full color. In terms of composition, lighting, and graphic texture it works in a substantially different way, and switching from color to monochrome calls for rethinking your visual approach.

By restricting the means of recording images to a range from white through grays to black, it gives special importance to the modulation of tones. This in turn gives stronger meaning to shape and line. With the image constructed entirely in grayscale, the viewer's eye pays more attention to texture, too. Black-and-white is capable of great subtlety. As a rule, scenes in which the main visual interest is in pattern, texture, silhouettes, or the contrast between different shapes, are candidates for thinking in black-and-white.

However, even if you have shot in color, you can still convert the image to mono-chrome by discarding color information. Better still, having the resource of all three color channels—red (R), green (G), and blue (B)—allows you to control the tonal values of an image with precision.

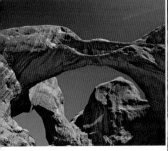
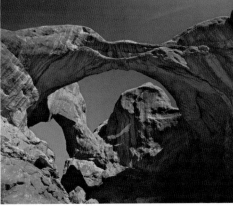

AUTOMATIC DESATURATION
The default methods of removing color in Photoshop are to choose either Grayscale from *Image>Mode* or Desaturate from *Image>Adjustments*. They have essentially the same result, which is to assign equal values of red, green, and blue to each pixel, and therefore offer little in the way of control.

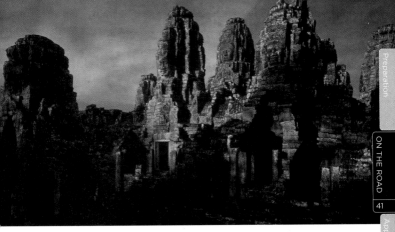

Preparation

ON THE ROAD

41

Appreciating Light

Subjects

Themes

Reference

MORE EVOCATIVE IN MONOCHROME
The rich complexity of shadows and the texture of carved stone at the temple of Bayon in Cambodia carry more weight without the distraction of color. Here, black-and-white allows the eye to savor tonal variety and subtle differences in the surfaces of the ruined monument.

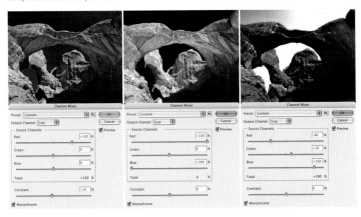

CHANNEL MIXER
By checking the Monochrome box of the Channel Mixer, you can adjust the channels and experiment with the tones of each element of the scene.

DARK RED
A high red value, and low blue one (comparable to using a dark red filter on the lens) darkens the sky and achieves an almost infrared effect.

STRONG BLUE
The high blue value cancels out blue in the image, with the result that the sky is made paler. In contrast, the yellow tones in the rocks become richer.

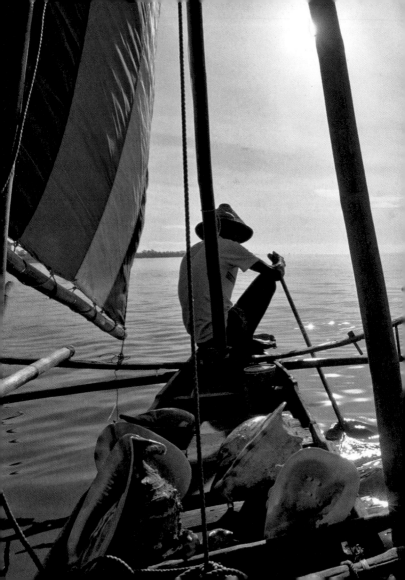

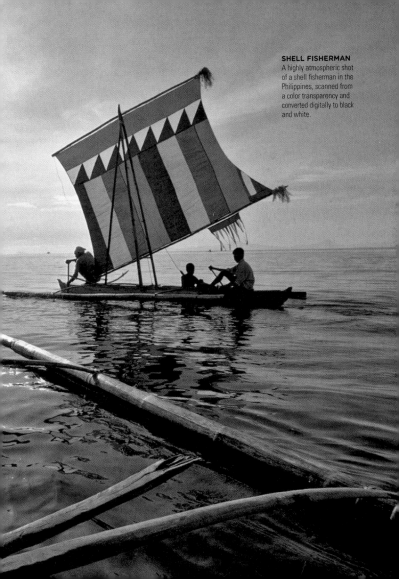

SHELL FISHERMAN
A highly atmospheric shot of a shell fisherman in the Philippines, scanned from a color transparency and converted digitally to black and white.

Panoramas

The term panorama is used for wide horizontal, mostly landscape, views. The long format, trimmed top and bottom, gives the eye a chance to roam around the picture. Just as in real life, you don't take in everything at a single glance. Instead, you discover different things within the picture, even if this takes only a few seconds.

A panoramic frame is surprisingly easy to use for composition. Even if the scene itself doesn't seem to be so horizontal, the frame can act like a storyboard, with things going on in different parts. It even works to have the frame "divided" into panel-like areas. It usually helps if you can include plenty of detail or events in the frame, so that the eye has every opportunity to explore.

What makes it so relevant to digital photography is the software available to join a strip of separate images into one seamless, almost endless view. This has proved so popular that digital camera manufacturers now routinely include a so-called "stitching" program on the software that usually accompanies the camara. There are also

specialist stitcher programs that simplify the precedure and offer advanced features. The one used here is Stitcher, but most stitching software works in the same way.

The sequence is simple. Begin with an overlapping horizontal of images shot from the same spot. The overlap should be at least one-third between each pair of frames. The stitching software needs to know this in order to find common points in neighboring images, to merge them. Select the images to be merged and the software will automatically create the panorama.

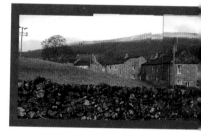

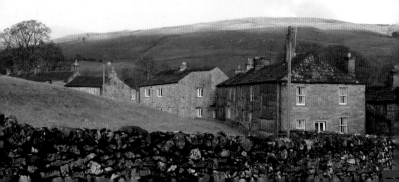

Preparation

ON THE ROAD

45

Appreciating Light

Subjects

Themes

Reference

Leveling the sequence

The best results for a single-strip panorama are when the camera is perfectly level. If not, you will lose some of the assembled image when cropping into a rectangle. Ideally, use a panoramic head featuring a level on a tripod, but it is also perfectly acceptable (and much easier) to shoot by hand. Keep the horizon at the same height in each frame.

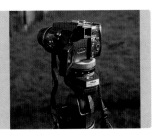

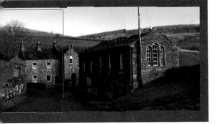

SHOOTING SEQUENCE
A sequence of five overlapping frames was taken. An overlap between each of about 40% helps the stitcher software to find enough corresponding points.

STITCHING
The images are loaded in order into the stitching program. This warps each to fit the others, then equalizes the tones for a smooth blend. Finally, it renders the panorama as a TIFF or JPEG file.

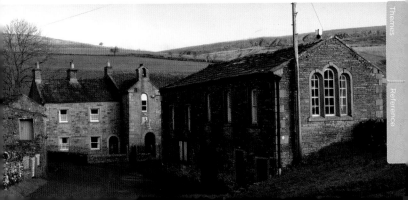

Cultural restrictions

Generally speaking, too much is made of differences in behavior between cultures. Crass is crass in most societies. As a rule, polite behavior works universally, and is no bad thing to exercise all the time.

However, photography, by its very nature, can be intrusive. Bear this in mind when in a different culture, as doing something which may be just acceptable in your own society—a slight breach of politeness that is nevertheless recoverable with a smile—may go too far elsewhere.

You will be forgiven minor cultural gaffes unless you have already managed to annoy people in other ways. Major ones should be obvious, but are outlined here in any case. The principal exception to all of this is in countries that are undergoing some periodic upheaval in their society, politics, or economy. A wave of religious fundamentalism, for example, may last just a few years, but during that time many people are likely to be highly sensitized to behavior that does not comply.

Customs

○ Footwear indoors: In many Buddhist countries, Japan (where the custom is only partly related to Buddhism), and some tribal societies, shoes should be removed before entering houses, places of worship, and some other interiors.

Social issues

○ Poverty: Scenes of people living in poverty reflect badly on the government. In some countries you may encounter objections.
○ Ethnicity: Some countries have internal racial problems, and this includes tribal conflict and minority peoples. Some minority people even quarantine themselves from outsiders, for example the Hopi in the southwestern USA.
○ Dress: Traditional dress, while actively celebrated at festivals and parades, may in some countries at some times be considered a sign of "backwardness." It is also, of course, connected to ethnicity problems and to religion.
○ Gender: In some societies with unequal rights between genders, you may encounter problems photographing women. Always ask beforehand.

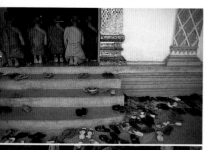

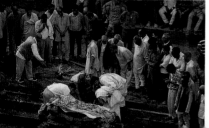

FOOTWEAR
Many Asian countries have a deeply ingrained custom of removing shoes in religious places and even in homes.

CREMATION
Open-air cremation is a Hindu custom. In general, don't photograph one. An exception here was the public cremation of a member of the Nepalese royal family.

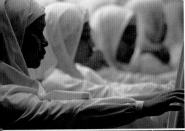

Preparation

ON THE ROAD

47

Appreciating Light

Subjects

Themes

Reference

MUSLIM SCHOOL
Girls in an Islamic school in Singapore. Religion and dress can together be a sensitive issue—again, it is essential to clear permission first.

POVERTY: INDIA
Part of a normal day on the streets in Old Delhi, but be aware that other people, in particular police, are likely to object if you spend too much time on shots like this.

○ Jewish: The stricter sects will not want to be photographed.
○ Sikh: In general Sikhs welcome non-Sikh visitors, and there may be only a few places where photography is prohibited.
○ Buddhist: As one of the world's most tolerant faiths, Buddhist sites are almost all open to photography.
○ Shinto: This Japanese faith places restrictions on entry and photography to the inner sanctuaries at the principal shrine, Isé. Otherwise, generally open.

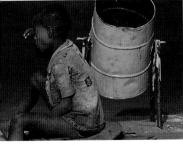

Religion

○ Christian: Few restrictions in mainstream Christianity, although sects tend by their nature to isolate themselves (Mennonites, for example). As with any religion, if you want to photograph inside a place of worship during prayers, mass, or any ceremony, ask first.
○ Muslim: Generally restrictive for photographs, in some places extremely so. Much depends on the country (Indonesia, for example, tends to be more relaxed than Pakistan), but it is wise to start from the assumption that photography may be banned in the interiors of mosques. Ask and you may be pleasantly surprised. In strict Muslim societies where women are veiled or otherwise shrouded, it is a good idea not to photograph them.
○ Hindu: As Hinduism is not a single unified religion, restrictions depend on the deity worshipped. In general, inner sanctuaries prohibit photography.

A few tips

- If in doubt, watch what other people do first. (Isn't that what your mother taught you at the dining table?)
- Smile a lot.
- Don't draw unnecessary attention to yourself.
- If you think you've really made a faux pas, move away.
- Don't display anger.
  Vent any of your frustrations later.
- Display good manners.
- Be polite and friendly.
- Learn a little of the language.

Editing your images

Editing photographs, by which here is meant the selection process of images to keep and images to throw out, has always been an integral part of the creative process. With film it was usually reserved for the return home, but now, digitally, images are available for viewing immediately, so that at the end of a day you can valuably review what you did.

Given an adequate viewing system, you can sit at the end of a day in a hotel room, and examine your images. By doing this you have an overview of the trip as it progresses, as well as valuable feedback on successes. It does, however, need a computer. If you travel with a laptop, good. Otherwise, on-the-road editing is one more factor to consider.

You can perform an immediate edit with the camera as long as the images are still on the memory card, but on a long trip you will have to download these—onto the hard drive of a laptop or a portable storage device. Some portable storage models allow viewing on a small screen, which is useful, but not particularly convenient for editing, which really needs images to be viewed side by side in groups.

The software for editing digital images is classified according to the sophistication of its features. Browsers are generally restricted to doing just that—viewing the stored images. All the camera manufacturers supply a browser to display images downloaded from the camera.

A step up from browsers are image management programs. These are able to order images in a variety of ways and provide the means to search and find images. As your collection increases, an image database becomes essential.

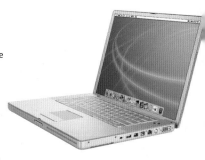

PORTABLE COMPUTER
Traveling with a laptop computer gives you plenty of storage space and functionality on the move.

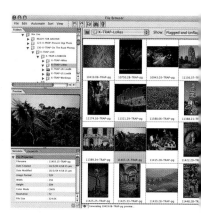

FILE BROWSER
This is Photoshop's File Browser. It displays thumbnails of any folder of image files, and any relevant information you choose, like size or resolution.

Digital rejects

One problem with on-the-spot editing is that it's actually too easy to throw images away. Until you reach the point of having no room whatsoever for storage, I recommend as a precaution that when you discard images during editing you place them in a special Rejects folder rather than fully delete them. You can revisit the folder later and delete then.

Basic editing procedure

Irrespective of where you do this, photo-editing invokes certain skills and sensibilities. Here are some basic things to think about:

- Throw out all technically incompetent shots (wrong exposure, blur, shake, etc.). By "throw out" I mean, of course, put in a Reject folder (see above).
- Discard images that are awkward, in the sense of a clumsy arrangement or moment, such as someone blinking.
- Group sequences and very similar images of the same subject.
- Mark or flag in some way (depending on your editing software) the best one or two images in each of the sequences, and the best among all the other images. These images are the "selects."
- If your editing software allows several folders or catalogues containing copies of the same image, open some with themes relevant to the trip, for example "People," "Landscapes," "Colors," "Markets." Place copies of appropriate images in these.

Portable printer

A valuable, unique tool for shooting in situations where goodwill is paramount, a portable digital printer makes it possible, at relatively low running costs, to supply the people around you with instant mementoes. In this sense, the portable printer can take the place of Polaroid prints. The only major drawback, as for Polaroids, is that once seen, everyone wants a print! This Canon CD-100 uses dye-sublimation, thermal transfer technology to produce 300 dpi 10 x 15cm digital photo prints with a protective coating. It can be powered by a rechargeable battery and with a car adaptor kit.

BROWSER PROCEDURE
In your browser of choice, use flagging/tagging to mark selects and other groups of images. These can then be displayed on their own either in the same folder or as copies in secondary folders dedicated to particular groupings.

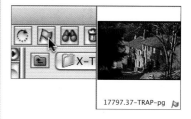

17797.37-TRAP-pg

Notes and captions

Why bother to keep notes? Surely this interrupts the creative flow of the shooting, besides being something of a chore. The answer lies in the nature of travel photography. Most travel photography is heavy on content—the what, who, and where of it all—and in traveling to new destinations there is always a lot to discover and learn. The name of this temple, the location of a hidden beach, the date and significance of a special ceremony: there is likely to be a constant stream of facts accompanying your photographs, and the details are normally available there and then. Noting them on the spot, either in a notebook or with a small tape recorder, will save a lot of trouble later trying to retrieve information that you have forgotten.

Photograph the label

In situations where objects are labeled, the easiest way to record the information is to take a shot of the label. Do this immediately after or before the main photograph, but be consistent as to which, particularly when shooting a series of objects, such as plants as in this example at a nursery.

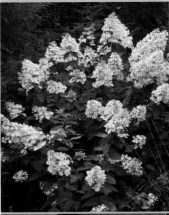

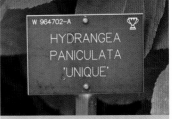

W 964702–A

HYDRANGEA
PANICULATA
'UNIQUE'

Keywords

If you want other people to be able to search through your library of pictures, for instance if you are selling them as stock photography, you will certainly have to anticipate how they might search. The answer lies in using keywords. These are words describing some aspect of an image; when someone enters a word in the search box of the database, the program will look for images that have the same word attached. The more varied yet apposite the set of keywords attached to each photograph, the better the chance of matching the searcher's request. The trick is in imagining what other people might look for, beyond the obvious description.

Captioning

For little extra effort, a caption can be attached
to a digital image so that it stays with it and is
always accessible. In the example below, essential
information is entered into File Info in Photoshop,
but the procedure is similar for other image-editing
programs. The windows have many entry fields,
but the three most important for photographers
are the copyright, the caption, and keywords.
All this information can be extracted by image-
management programs and other databases.

IPTC METADATA
Lengthy caption entries, including keywords and
copyright notice, are accessible in Photoshop
under *File > File Info…* Clicking Advanced allows
descriptions to be saved and appended—useful
if you have a number of images needing the
same caption.

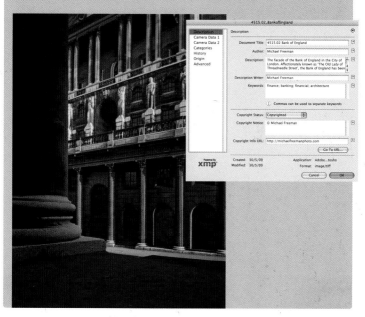

APPRECIATING LIGHT

The quality of light brings so much to the character of a photograph, and much will depend on the location, the time of year, and the time of day. If your travels have taken you to a previously unvisited destination, and an "exotic" one at that, in all likelihood you will find the quality of light and the way it behaves during the course of a day very different from your experiences at home. While this may take a couple of days to adjust to, you'll soon be appreciating the opportunities it affords you.

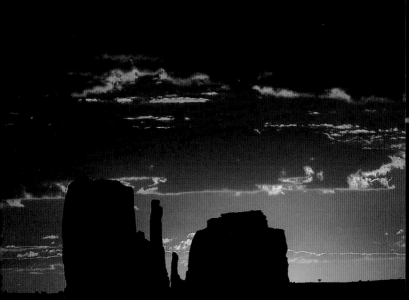

Preparation

On the road

APPRECIATING
LIGHT

53

Subjects

Themes

Reference

For general outdoor shooting, probably the most favored natural light for photographers is moderately low sunlight, as at midmorning and midafternoon. This is the lighting that dominates, for instance, travel brochures. Variations and extensions of this are when the sun is quite close to the horizon, although here the shooting window is much shorter, which means fewer images. The reason for the commercial popularity of bright-sun-but-not-too-high light is that this is tourist weather—the conditions in which most people like to travel for pleasure.

Some photographers, however, think that you can have too much of a good, or at least a predictable, thing. Certainly, given the constant demands of publishing and advertising to come up with striking, different new images, travel photographers are under pressure to find different light treatments. The aesthetics of "nice lighting" are, after all, quite fashionable. And fashions change.

In this section, we'll look in detail not only at how light behaves and the effect it will have on your photographs during the course of a day—from sunrise to sunset—but also how this behavior and resulting impact on photography is governed by where your are in the world. In addition, it's also important to understand of the significance of the direction of light in relation to the subject—whether the subject is lit from behind, from the side, or from the front—as this will drastically alter the quality of the image.

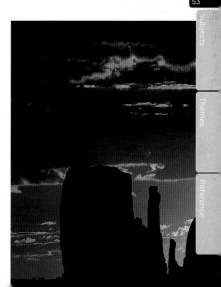

EXACTLY SUNRISE
Sunrise photography depends on clear air for the full red effect, but the moment lasts just a few minutes. Sunrise is often most effective when used for a silhouette, as with the rock formations known as The Mittens in Monument Valley.

Climate and light

Natural light depends on weather, which depends in turn on the climate. Traveling makes you more conscious of this, partly because you are likely to be more exposed to outdoor conditions than usual, and partly because you are likely to be in a less familiar climate (this depends, of course, on how far you have traveled). World travel is now so much easier, cheaper, and more common than it was, say, twenty years ago, that more and more of us are experiencing very different climates on our trips. There are a dozen major climatic zones (including mountains as one) according to the standard classification, but of course there are rarely sharp divides between them. Microclimates also add variety.

Although I'm stressing the effect that climates have on light, there is also sometimes the more practical matter of accessibility. Climates that have extreme seasons may also

KEY	Color	Precipitation	Temperature & conditions
Arctic	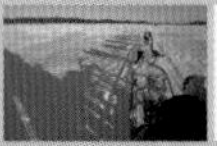	None	Cold
Subarctic	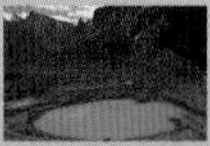	Snow	Very cold, permafrost
Cold, snowy	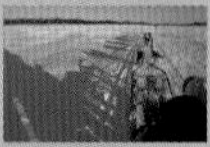	Rain/Snow	Below 26°F (−3°C) in winter
Temperate	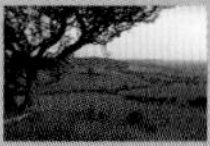	Seasonal	Above 26°F (−3°C) in winter
Mountain	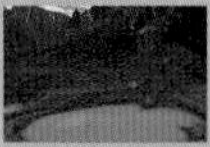	Various	Altitude dependent
Dry	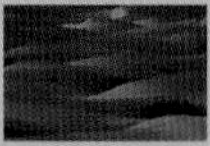	Below 10 in (250 mm)/year	Hot or cold
Tropical	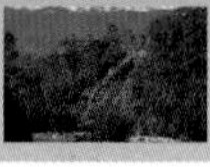	Heavy	Rainfall heavy, often all year

make it difficult to get around, particularly in less-developed places. The wet season in a monsoonal country like Cambodia, for example, turns most of the roads to mud, and this drastically restricts the areas of the country you can visit. The summer in the Sudan brings the possibility of the *haboob*, a huge, sudden duststorm that can travel at speeds of 50 mph (80 km/h) with a front wall of up to 3,000 ft (900 m). These kinds of climatic detail call for very specific research;

use the climate maps and descriptions that follow as an introduction and general guide, but for your exact destination do some in-depth research.

Finally, there's the issue of comfort. Shooting outdoors at 104˚F (40˚C) is no joke, and will slow most people down. Very low temperatures also take up time and energy—removing gloves, unzipping jackets, avoiding frostbite, and so on. Remember to factor this in.

Preparation

On the road

APPRECIATING LIGHT

55

Subjects

Themes

Reference

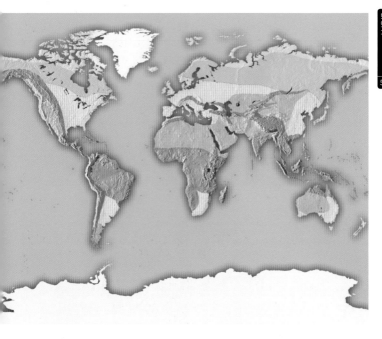

Tropical light

Tropical wet

Monotonous and sultry, with no seasons and little variation in the heat and rainfall, both of which are high. Never cool, and while average temperatures are around 80°F (26°C), it feels hotter and more enervating because of the high humidity. Most of the rainfall is convectional, typically late in the afternoon as thunderstorms, with squalls. Often cloudy, but mornings start off bright.

Examples: The Amazon, Borneo, New Guinea.

Lighting issues: Sun intense when it appears. Probability of sunrises, and sunsets if there has been a late-afternoon thunderstorm to clear the air. Midday sun overhead and difficult for shooting. Rains heavy, but usually brief. Spectacular cloud formations from convectional rain.

Equipment issues: High heat and humidity are potentially damaging. Heavy rains demand very good protection.

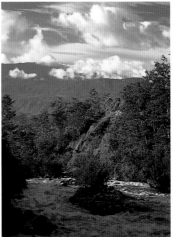

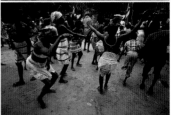

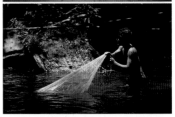

IRIAN JAYA
An equatorial climate is not all rain, even if hot and sticky. Early and late, as here in the Baliem Valley, the light can be rich and the cloud formations often piled high.

SURINAM
A village ceremony in the interior of this South American country, typically overcast but much brighter than equivalent weather in a temperate climate.

BORNEO
Midday sun on the equator is harsh, and in shaded locations like this, the contrast is so high that shadow details are inevitably lost.

Preparation

On the road

APPRECIATING
LIGHT

57

Subjects

Themes

Reference

Tropical monsoon

A variation on Tropical wet in that rainfall is concentrated in one definite season—the monsoon—which often breaks on one particular day. There are commonly three seasons: rainy (during which there are still some drier, sunny periods), followed by cool dry, which gradually changes into hot dry.

Examples: Indo-China, most of India.

Lighting issues: Seasonality makes the timing of a trip critical. The best sunshine is immediately following the monsoon, but skies can be unremittingly blue and therefore ultimately boring. The dry period before the monsoon can be hazy. How heavy and continuous the monsoon rains are depends on the region.

Equipment issues: For the rainy season, see opposite (Tropical wet). The end of the dry season can be very hot.

THAILAND
The more familiar light is the clear, often cloudless skies of the dry monsoon in the cool season—crisp in the early morning and late afternoon, but with a certain monotony of blue sky.

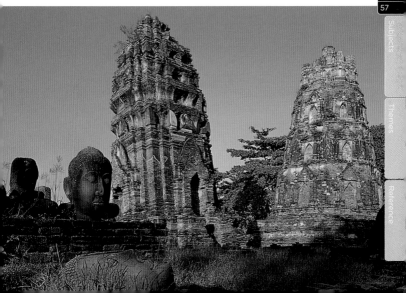

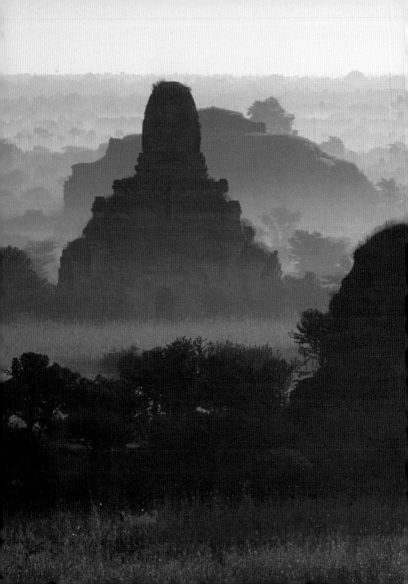

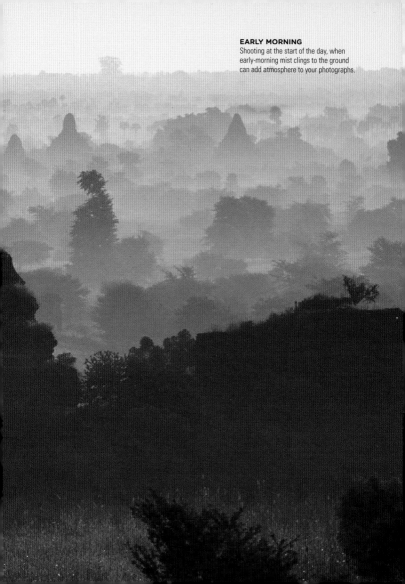

EARLY MORNING
Shooting at the start of the day, when early-morning mist clings to the ground can add atmosphere to your photographs.

Light in dry climates

Savannah

Another tropical climate, with less overall rainfall than the previous two, and a long, distinctly dry season. These conditions result in large areas of grassland instead of forest. A rainy season is followed by a cool dry season, becoming hot dry.

Examples: East Africa, the Guiana Highlands.

Lighting issues: Dry season is light, bright, and clear, with particularly good visibility in upland areas like East Africa. Rainy season offers variable light, not as heavily overcast as in Tropical monsoon regions.

Equipment issues: Dust is the main problem in the dry season.

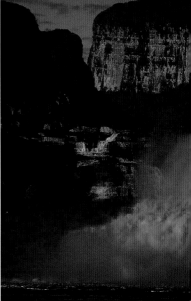

GUIANA HIGHLANDS
The high savannah of southern Venezuela in May, which is the start of the hot season (although the height of the base plateau at around 4,900 ft (1,500 m) keeps the temperatures bearable). Generally clear skies, and dry.

SOUTH AFRICA
Rhino capture in the Pilanesberg National Park, near Sun City, South Africa. May in the southern hemisphere is winter, and at over 3,300 ft (1,000 m) this plateau area is crisp, cool, and dry. High UV-content gives shadows and distances a bluish cast.

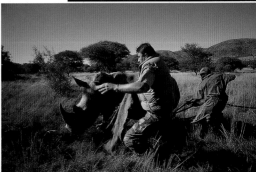

Preparation

On the road

APPRECIATING LIGHT

61

Subjects

Themes

Reference

Semi-arid steppe

A dry climate with low, irregular, and undependable rainfall. Drought years are interspersed with years of moderate rain, but are hard to predict. In the tropics, summer is hot and winter cool, but further north, as in the Asian steppes, the temperature range is greater, with hot summers and cold winters. Rainfall distribution by month varies from region to region, but is always unreliable.

Examples: Afghanistan, northern New Mexico.

Lighting issues: High percentage of clear skies, and in the driest season often no cloud for days at a time, giving solid blue skies.

Equipment issues: Needs protection against dust.

Desert

Rainfall is usually less than 10 in (250 mm), and in extreme places like the Atacama in northern Chile there may be no rain at all for years on end. Very reliable sunshine, and hence great temperature variation from day (very hot) to night (cool to cold). Duststorms possible, and in some desert areas these are seasonal and sometimes predictable. Coastal deserts experience fog, mist, and sometimes low cloud.

Examples: The Sahara, Namibia.

Lighting issues: Intense sun, blue skies. Early mornings and afternoons are key times for outside shooting.

Equipment issues: Extremes of heat and dust. Very sharp drop in temperature at night can cause condensation problems.

NEW MEXICO
Dry conditions predominate in the southwest, as here in Santa Fe, New Mexico. Clear, bright days are predictable for much of the year, accounting for its long popularity with painters and photographers.

DEATH VALLEY
Below sea level at some points, Death Valley in California experiences an average of 2 in (50 mm) of rain a year and the highest mean temperatures in the US—and the highest record of 134°F (56.7°C). It has four areas of sand dune.

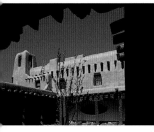

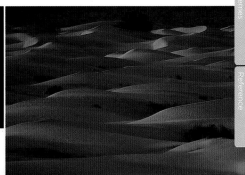

Mid-latitude light

Mediterranean

Probably the most comfortable, attractive climate for general photography. Rainfall is low and concentrated in the mild winter season, leaving the summers bright, sunny, and warm-to-hot. Some coastal locations, like San Francisco, have cool summers and significant fog in the mornings.

Examples: The Mediterranean coast, central California.

Lighting issues: High sunshine percentage and high reliability. Easy to schedule shooting in advance.

Equipment issues: No special problems.

Humid subtropical

Cool winters, hot summers, with moderately high rainfall that is either throughout the year or concentrated in part of the summer. High summer humidity makes the height of this season uncomfortable and muggy. Liable to hurricanes and typhoons (same thing, different name) in late summer and early fall.

Examples: The US Gulf States, central and southern Japan.

Lighting issues: Variety of lighting conditions, low-to-moderate predictability.

Equipment issues: In summer, heat and humidity can be as high as in Tropical wet regions.

NEW ORLEANS
Hot, steamy, but bright—early morning in the French Quarter of New Orleans on the Mississippi.

AEGEAN
A whitewashed Greek church against an intense blue sky on the island of Mykonos is archetypical of the Mediterranean ideal.

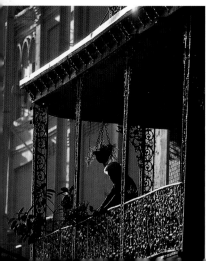

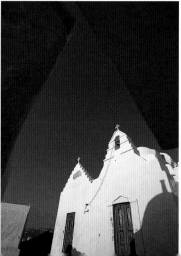

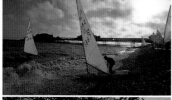

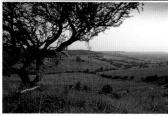

Preparation

On the road

APPRECIATING LIGHT

63

Subjects

Themes

Reference

ENGLAND
While the English weather is actually very varied, a blustery day like this, with a mixture of sunshine and showers, is widely considered typical.

ENGLAND
The type of weather that draws the most complaints in marine climates like that of Western Europe is overcast, when depressions arriving from a long sea crossing can bring day after day of featureless, gray light.

Marine

Summers cool to warm, winters never very cold. Rainfall is fairly high, but varies greatly from region to region, spread across the year but less in the summer. Unpredictability of everything is characteristic, and for photography this can be difficult. Weather is dominated by air coming in off the ocean, more often than not as depressions.

Examples: Western Europe, Vancouver, Washington State.

Lighting issues: Highly variable weather and difficult to predict. The light can change even several times in one day. Distance from equator causes a strong seasonal difference in the height of the sun and the length of the day.

Equipment issues: No special problems.

Continental

Severe differences in temperature between the seasons, with warm-to-hot summers and cold winters—annual temperature ranges of around 50°F (10°C) are common. Precipitation across the year with a summer maximum; many snow-covered days in the winter.

Examples: The continental US and parts of central Europe.

Lighting issues: Length of daylight and height of the sun are similar to marine climates. Conditions moderately predictable.

Equipment issues: Severe winters can give subarctic conditions.

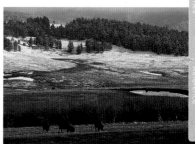

Arctic and mountain light

Subarctic

Huge area of the Earth's surface but very small population. Long, bitterly cold winters, very short summers, brief spring and fall. Summer days are long, winter very short. Low precipitation concentrated in warmer months, but long-lasting snow cover in winter.

Examples: The Russian taiga, much of Canada and Alaska.

Lighting issues: Very long daylight hours in summer allows extended shooting, but very short days in winter are restrictive. The sun is never high, so clear weather very attractive. As with Arctic regions, possibility of aurora borealis.

Equipment issues: Cold and condensation are the main problems.

Arctic and Antarctic

Never warm and the winters are bitterly cold. The main feature for photography is continuous light in summer and continuous darkness in winter. Tundra is the part bordering the ice caps.

Examples: Greenland, Antarctica.

Lighting issues: By definition, winters are essentially one long night, although one special feature is the aurora borealis. Summer days move from one long sunrise to one slow sunset, with the sun's path traveling around the horizon.

Equipment issues: Severe cold.

LAPLAND

The winter of northern Sweden is characterized by snow cover and Arctic conditions—sometimes as benign as this clear afternoon from a dogsled.

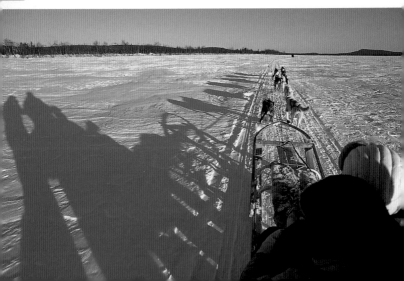

Mountain

Mountains intrude so much into the surrounding climates that they create their own general group of climates. It varies greatly, and in any one region is arranged vertically. As a rule of thumb, above about 5,000 ft (1,500 m), mountains create their own climates. It is difficult to generalize, but characteristics are low pressure, high UV, and intense sunlight, leading to high contrast in both light and temperature between sun and shade. Thin air gives a high temperature range from day to night, also. Precipitation is often higher than in the surrounding lowlands because the mountains cause air to rise and lose its capacity to hold moisture. Often this is on the windward side only, while the lee stays drier. There may be special mountain and valley winds.

Examples: The Rockies, the Himalayas.

Lighting issues: High altitude means strong UV and so blue distances and shadows. Thin air gives high contrast in sunlight, so expose for lit areas, not shadows. Weather often unpredictable, so light can change rapidly according to cloud cover.

Equipment issues: Physical protection against knocks is a priority, particularly when climbing is involved. High altitude means possibility of cold and condensation problems, especially at night.

HIMALAYAS

At 16,400 ft (5,000 m), the visibility in fine weather is exceptionally good—the atmosphere is thinner than at sea-level, with 50% of the oxygen. The strong blues are due to the correspondingly high UV content.

HIMALAYAS

Weather, light, and temperature shifts can be rapid and distinct at these altitudes (here, in western Tibet, at 19,700 ft/6,000 m). Clouds passing in front of the sun change the lighting more dramatically than at sea-level because of the greater difference between light and shade.

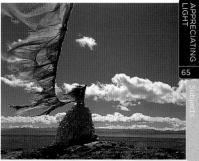

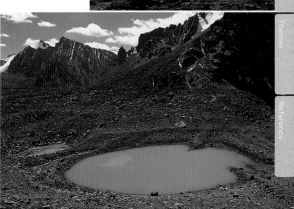

Preparation

On the road

APPRECIATING LIGHT

65

Subjects

Themes

Reference

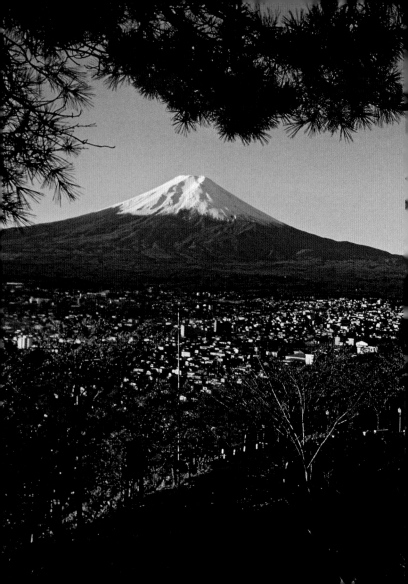

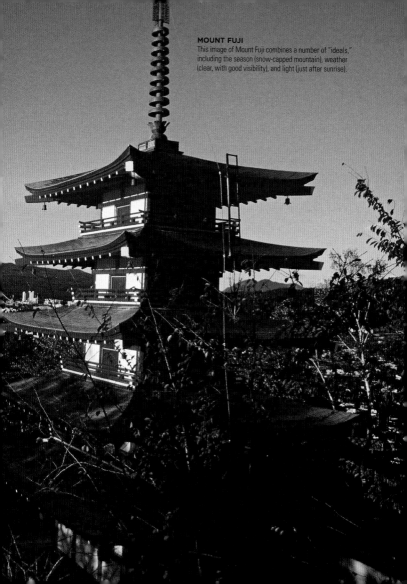

MOUNT FUJI
This image of Mount Fuji combines a number of "ideals," including the season (snow-capped mountain), weather (clear, with good visibility), and light (just after sunrise).

Middle of the day

From late morning through to early afternoon (the exact times will vary depending on latitude and the time of the year) the sun is high in the sky. Many photographers regard this time of day as providing the least appealing light, and there are good reasons for this. However, it's not necessarily time to put away your camera and wait for more photogenic lighting conditions.

When the sun is high in the sky, shadows are very short. With little or no discernible shadow, landscapes will not benefit from the modeling effect (which helps to emphasize undulating form) that is apparent when the sun is lower in the sky and any shadows cast are a great deal longer. Furthermore, if the sun is strong (and it will be at its strongest at this time of day), many scenes will have high contrast and a very wide dynamic range, making it difficult to capture detail in both highlight and shadow regions. This can often result in images that are difficult to "read," with dark shadows and bright highlights obscuring important, "signposting" detail.

Photographing people when the sun is high in the sky also has its drawbacks. Your subject's eyes will usually be cast in shadow (either by the subject's own forehead and eyebrows), his or her nose may well appear ungainly, while the harsh light itself is not particularly flattering on certain skin colors.

Setting aside these technical drawbacks, high sun also has a reputation for producing bland, unexciting images. If you flick through a series of photographs, it's likely that the ones that grab your attention most are those in which the light is dramatic or unusual. With its consistency in terms of light levels and quality, high sun is rarely striking.

What, then, does midday light have to recommend it? Well its greatest asset is that it can produce crisp, clear images, particularly when the air is clean. Shapes are clearly defined and colors are accurately and brightly rendered. And while horizontal subjects don't benefit from any modeling effect, vertical surfaces, on the other hand, benefit from raking shadows, which help emphasize form and texture.

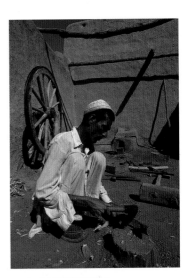

HOLDING THE HIGHLIGHTS
The contrast range in this shot of a Pathan craftsman was high at about 6 stops: the highlight reading, taken from his shoulder, was f/32; the shadow reading, taken from his neck, was f/4. However, his white clothes are such an important part of the image that they control the exposure setting; overexposure would be unacceptable. This exposure gives deep shadows, but the viewpoint was chosen so as to keep these small.

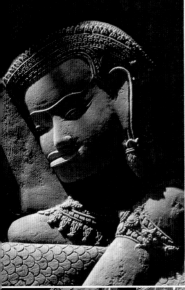

VERTICAL SURFACES

A high sun gives raking light on walls and other vertical surfaces, and, in the case of important texture such as the bas-relief here, can be extremely useful. The effects shift rapidly, however, so timing is critical. As the sun passes over a building, the light leaves one wall and passes to the opposite.

GRAPHIC PATTERN

Bright, clear weather adds to the complexity of this street corner in Jaipur, India, by throwing extremely dense shadows. The stark, graphic effect produced is visually interesting in itself.

Preparation

On the road

APPRECIATING LIGHT

69

Subjects

Themes

Reference

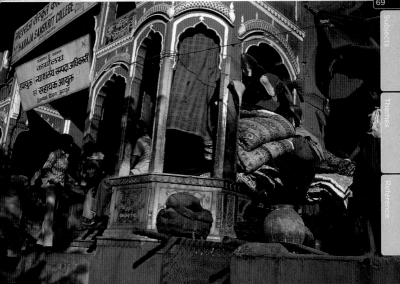

Morning and afternoon

The quality of light during the morning and afternoon, when the sun is lower in the sky, is favored by many photographers. The oblique angle of the sunlight, combined with the extra distance it has to travel through the atmosphere, is flattering for most subjects—shadows are less harsh and the softer, warmer light can introduce a pleasing glow to people's skin, making it an ideal time for portraits. For landscapes and many architectural shots, the low angle introduces that all-important modeling effect which helps to define the scene.

At the same time, although less dramatic than the light at dawn and dusk, there is less chance of an orange color cast, and the light can be relied on to produce neutral results if accurate colors are important.

At these times of day the photographer is also able to experiment with the position of the camera in relation to the sun. Shooting into the sun, with the light behind, or to one side, are all possible, and will produce very different results, each of which is covered in more detail later on.

Finally, a low sun is less harsh than that at midday, resulting in scenes with less dynamic range, making it easier for the camera to capture detail in both highlights and shadows.

SHOOTING DOWN

An overhead camera position can be a good option in morning or afternoon light. In this case, the contrast is usually much less because of the ground, or whatever surface the subject is resting on, but the texture remains strong. In addition, the long shadows make for interesting graphic compositions.

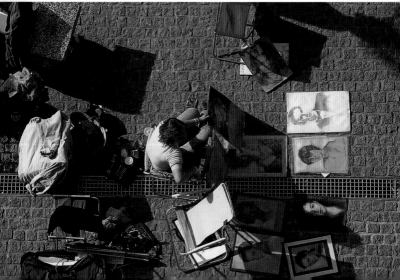

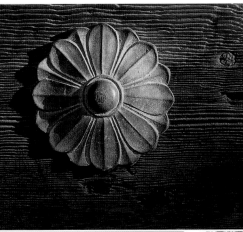

WALL DETAILS

Cross-lighting reveals texture at its strongest. Just as some vertical surfaces receive this at midday, others are at their best early and late in the day, as with this bronze fitting on a wooden wall. Here, the window of opportunity lasted only a few minutes before the shadows covered everything.

HORIZONTAL LIGHT AND SHADE

The visual play between highlights and shadows is an important component of photographs taken at these times of day. Shooting at right angles to the sun makes the most of this effect, and adds a linear, horizontal component to the image.

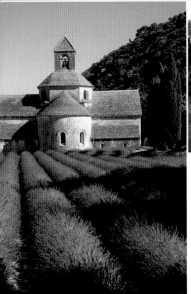

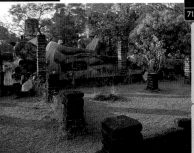

USING SHADOWS

The shapes cast by shadows when the sun is fairly low can be put to good graphic use. In this morning shot of an old French abbey with a garden of lavender, the foreground shadow makes a solid base for the composition; the middle-ground shadows of trees suggest the unseen forest at right; and the shadow cast by the conical roof continues the lines of the hill beyond.

Preparation

On the road

APPRECIATING LIGHT

71

Subjects

Themes

Reference

Sunrise and sunset

Images shot at sunrise or sunset can produce dramatic results, but it's very important to do some homework, particularly if you have a specific location in mind. You may, for example, come across a breathtaking scene during the day which would be enhanced by capturing it at sunrise. Yet having taken the trouble to get up early in good time to catch the sunrise, you find that the sun is in the wrong position and all the wonderful detail that was apparent during the day is obscured by flat, dark shadows. Scout your locations in advance and work out in which direction the sun will rise. You may find that although the scene is not suitable for a dawn shot, it does lend itself to a sun set.

With the sun so low in the sky, you'll find that the scene is actually darker than it appears, as our eyes are so good at adjusting to the available light. Always take a tripod and shutter release cable, or alternatively find something suitably sturdy on which to rest the camera. Although the sun may not be particularly strong, there is still likely to be a wide dynamic range throughout the scene, particularly if you're shooting into the sun. Take a reading from the sky with the sun just out of view. Recompose and take the shot. Check the histogram and highlight warning screen to ensure there aren't too many blown highlights and that dark areas of the image still retain detail. If necessary adjust the exposure and take another shot.

WARM, RICH COLOR
Exceptionally clear air keeps the sun bright, even when it is on the horizon and at its reddest, as in this shot of Monument Valley. The strongest colors appear with the sun behind you and the camera. You can avoid the problem of showing your own shadow by positioning yourself so that it falls in the distance, not on foreground features.

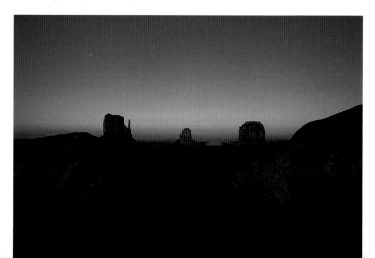

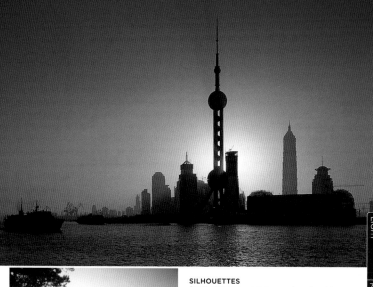

Preparation

On the road

APPRECIATING LIGHT

73

Subjects

Themes

Reference

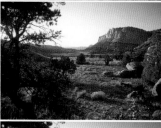

SILHOUETTES

Shooting into the sun as it rises or sets creates obvious opportunities for silhouettes. These are easiest with a wide-angle lens, which makes the image of the sun small, and so easy to hide behind a feature such as this Shanghai tower.

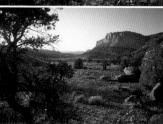

WATCH THE WHITE BALANCE

Make sure that the camera's white balance is set so that it does not compensate for the warm tones of a low sun, or the image will look strangely unsunset-like. This happened with an Auto setting (above left), in contrast to a straightforward Direct Sun setting (left).

Twilight

Twilight is the relatively short period of time that exists just before the sun has risen over the horizon or just after it has set. Exactly how long this lasts is down to your latitude, while how the sky appears will depend on the atmospheric conditions. If the sky is clear, you'll be rewarded with a smooth gradation of color, starting with warm reds and oranges surrounding the sun, gradually fading to the cooler violets and blues, and eventually to black.

As with sunrise and sunset, it pays to get to your location early, which if you're shooting at the beginning of the day may well mean arriving while it is still dark. So plan your trip in advance and assemble all of your equipment before going to bed! Exposures are likely to be relatively long, so you'll need a tripod and remote shutter release.

With the sun actually out of view, you need to consider carefully your white balance setting. If you're shooting Raw, which is recommended no matter what lighting conditions you're working under, the white balance setting is less of an issue; if, however, you're shooting JPEGs (perhaps with a view to printing directly) experiment with the setting until you get the result you're happy with. The lower (or cooler) the setting, say around 2800K, will result in cooler, bluer images, which reinforce the tones commonly found at these times of day.

In terms of composition, remember that you're going to be using exposures as long as perhaps 30 seconds. You can use this to your advantage. The movement of waves, for example, under long exposures takes on a smooth, cloudy appearance, while car lights can create attractive light trials.

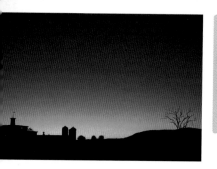

SHADING OF THE SKY
A clear sky at dusk or dawn acts like a smooth reflective surface for the sun as it lies below the horizon. The light shades smoothly upward from the horizon, and this effect is most obvious with a wide-angle lens, which takes in a greater span of sky. For example, while a 180 mm telephoto lens gives a limited angle of view of only 11 degrees, a 20 mm wide-angle lens gives an angle of view of 84 degrees.

Wide-angle or telephoto?

Experiment with both wide-angle and telephoto lenses, or both ends of the zoom range. Wide-angle views take in more of the height of the sky and capture a wide range of color. Telephoto shots, with a narrower angle of view, can only take in a small part of this; perhaps only a single color.

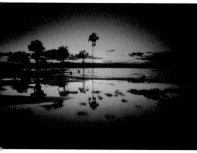

Preparation

On the road

APPRECIATING LIGHT

75

Subjects

Themes

Reference

REFLECTIONS AT DUSK
Shooting from almost at water level enhances the delicate
tonal gradation before night falls over the Guiana Highlands
of Venezuela. What makes this view attractive is that almost
all the color has been drained from the scene.

BLUE INTENSITY
When the sky is not red or orange at sunset or sunrise,
an overall blue cast is typical, as in this winter scene.

Clouds at twilight

Added to the basic lighting condition, clouds are
fairly unpredictable in their effect. If continuous,
they usually destroy any sense of twilight, but if
broken, they reflect light dramatically: high orange
and red clouds create the classic "postcard"
sunset. One of the things that becomes clear after
a number of occasions is that clouds at this time
of day often produce surprises. The upward angle
of the sunlight from below the horizon is acute to
the layers of clouds, so that small movements
have obvious effects. On some occasions, the
color of clouds after sunset simply fades; on
others, it can suddenly spring to life again for
a few moments—a good argument for not
packing up as soon as the sun has set.

Keep shooting

After the sun has set, even when you think you've
captured the image that you had in mind from the
outset, keep shooting if there's any light at all left
to shoot by—shooting in twilight is full of surprises
and you never really know when the light has
gone for good. You might think it's all over only to
discover a full moon rising, and a whole new set
of possibilities opening up to you.

Rain and storms

With the onset of rain, particularly if it's heavy, many photographers will pack up their equipment and head for home. This is understandable—it's no fun getting soaking wet, especially if it's cold, and rainwater can damage expensive cameras and lenses.

However, if you can find shelter that will keep you and your equipment dry, and which still provides access to a photogenic scene, it's worth continuing to photograph. Rain can create very evocative images and pleasing alternatives to sundrenched landscapes. Light levels are usually low and a gentle, shadowless light can often bring out certain colors to great advantage, noticeably greens. Plant foliage, for example, will reproduce well in rainy conditions.

If your intention is to capture the essence of rain it's rarely worth attempting to photograph the rain itself—unless it is strongly backlit against a very dark background the rain won't be clearly visible. Instead, use a medium-to-long telephoto lens to zoom into a specific object that shows the rain—an overflowing drain, rivulets running down a street, raindrops on the end of a leaf—all these will illustrate the rain much more effectively than a blurry looking scene.

With rainstorms can often come lightning. If captured well, lightning can add great drama to a landscape or cityscape. It's easier to capture lightning in dark conditions, so to begin with don't try photographing lightning during the day or in very bright ambient lighting conditions. The secret to good lightning shots lies in knowing where and when the lightning will strike. Most lightning will center around thunderstorms, and it's likely that where the first lightning strike occurred, others will follow. Set the

camera on a tripod and use a wide-angle lens to cover a good area of the scene in which the first bolts appeared. Set the camera to Manual and turn Autofocus off. Set focus to Infinity, set the aperture to around f/8, and the shutter to Bulb (B). Using a cable release, hold the shutter open until the next lightning strike. If you're in really dark conditions you can keep the shutter open for a minute or so and you may get a number of strikes recorded in one exposure. Review the images, and change either the aperture or the length of time you keep the shutter open to improve the lighting in your shots.

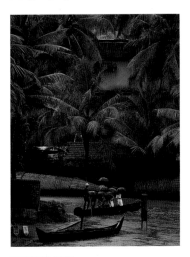

MONSOON HAZE
In this shot of a typical south Indian day during the monsoon, the rain is heavy yet appears like a dull haze. However, the people sheltering beneath umbrellas underline the reality of a rainstorm.

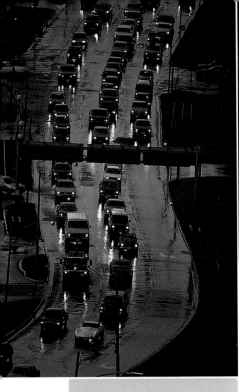

Preparation

On the road

APPRECIATING LIGHT

77

Subjects

Themes

Reference

CAPTURING LIGHTNING
Distant lightning over Rangoon was shot at dusk with a 30-second exposure—long enough to catch a few cloud-to-cloud strikes and one cloud-to-ground strike. The aperture was f/2.8 and the sensitivity ISO 100.

RAIN EFFECTS
To establish "raininess," some visual clues can help if you include them deliberately. In this shot, the reflections of car headlights in the wet surface of a Toronto freeway make the point effectively.

Stay safe

Lightning can kill. If you're at all concerned you're going to get struck:

• Get into a car or building.
• Crouch low to the ground, sitting on your heels.
• DO NOT take shelter under a large isolated tree.
• Avoid tall structures, such as towers, power or telephone lines, and high fences.
• If you feel your hair standing on end, this is a sign that lightning is about to strike. Drop any metal objects and crouch down with your hands on your knees.

Sidelighting

Of the three main lighting directions—backlighting, frontal lighting, and sidelighting (all of which we are going to discuss in the following pages), it is the latter that is widely considered the most dramatic. The drama inherent to sidelighting lies in the close relationship between highlights and shadows.

In sidelit scenes, when the light strikes the subject or scene at right angles in relation to the position of the camera, areas of shadow and highlights are more or less evenly distributed—think of a person's face lit purely from one side, half is in shade and half is lit. In this way sidelighting creates powerful, high-contrast images. This can be most effective if the background is in shade, as in the image of the two women below.

The distinctive shadows common to sidelighting have two further effects. First, they help to create a sense of depth to an image. Any object is represented twice in the photograph, first by itself and second by its shadow. This helps to create and reinforce a three-dimensional appearance within the photograph. Second, shadows cast by sidelighting tend to be long, and this helps to emphasize subject texture, as shown in the photograph of the Chinese lantern on the opposite page.

SHARP OUTLINE
One of the most effective uses of sidelighting to outline a subject depends almost entirely on the camera viewpoint. In this shot, taken in a Montreal park, the sun is at right angles to the view, and the background is in shadow.

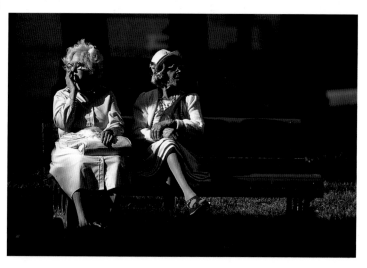

Getting the exposure right

In the vast majority of sidelighting situations it's much better to expose for the highlights. Use the spot or center-weighted metering mode if your camera has either, and recompose the photograph as necessary. The image won't be successful if any of the highlight areas are blown out (and these are likely to comprise at least some of the subject). If, however, detail is lost in some of the shadow areas, (which is only likely to happen under the brightest conditions), the effect has a much smaller impact on the viewer, and in many cases will only add to the drama of the image.

Preparation

On the road

APPRECIATING LIGHT

79

Subjects

Themes

Reference

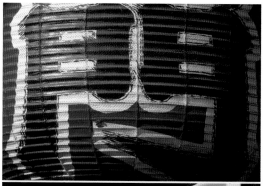

LIGHT AND TEXTURE
The angle of this Japanese lantern's paper surface changes gradually from left to right, and this affects the amount and distribution of shadow. The strongest impression of textural detail is when the sunlight grazes the surface at a very acute angle. Broadly speaking, there are three areas of texture detail, with light readings as follows:
left = f/16; center = f/11; right = f/4. The area of maximum texture detail is in the center.

RAKING LIGHT
In this shot of a yoghurt dish, photographed from directly above, sidelighting establishes the texture—an essential quality in food photography, where any tactile sensation helps to stimulate taste.

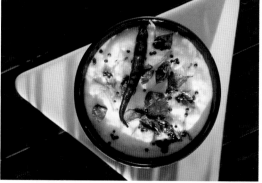

Frontal lighting

With the sun behind the photographer, and the light falling directly onto the subject, the subject is said to be front lit. As with the other varieties of lighting, frontal lighting has positive and negative points, so it's important to know what to look for when photographing front-lit scenes in order to capture a successful image.

The biggest drawback to frontally lit scenes is that, with the sun directly behind the photographer, shadows are thrown away from the camera, and, depending on the viewpoint, may not be visible at all. While on the one hand the lack of shadows is likely to ensure that the scene is evenly lit, making it easy to capture the image without fear of blowing out highlights, it does have one major drawback. Without shadows to emphasize texture, help with perspective,

and enhance modeling, front-lit subjects can appear flat and two-dimensional.

For this reason, successful frontally lit images, rather than relying on subtlety of texture or far-reaching perspective and depth, instead need subjects that have strong color and tone, and/or interesting outline form. Furthermore, if the sun is low in the sky the color temperature will also be low, imbuing everything with a warm yellow-orange tone, which can add contrast to color and tone. Look out, also, for reflective surfaces (although not so brightly reflective that they are in danger of blowing out). Such surfaces will leap out of the scene, particularly if surrounded by dark, non-reflective colors. The image of the Japanese woman shown here is a good example.

RICHNESS OF COLOR
The contrast between the black silk and gold embroidery is already strong. Frontal lighting enhances this by illuminating the glossy embroidery as strongly as possible.

FLAT GRAPHICS
The lack of shadows when the sun is directly on the camera axis can work well with strongly colored or contrasting subjects if you treat the composition as two-dimensional, ignoring perspective and depth.

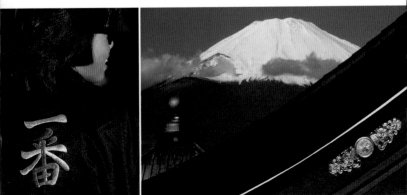

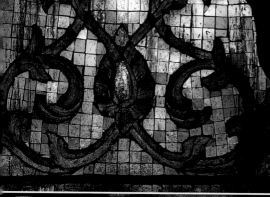

MIRRORED CONTRAST

Shooting straight into a highly reflecting surface, such as this mosaic of mirrors, will give extremely high contrast, so that any matt surfaces appear almost as silhouettes.

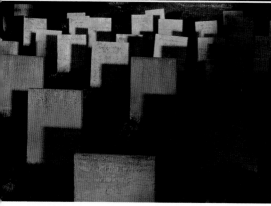

SHADOW SHAPES

Narrow but hard shadows from a setting sun almost behind the camera play an important part in a view of a Shaker cemetery near Albany, New York. It was necessary to position the camera carefully to prevent its shadow from appearing in the photograph.

Your shadow

The closer the sun sinks to the horizon, the longer shadows become—provided of course that the sun remains relatively bright. Although this can help create dramatic landscapes strewn with interesting and eye-catching shadowy forms, if you're shooting with the sun behind you it may be that one of those eye-catching shadows is the one cast by you and your tripod—a shadow that you could really do without in your photo. If this happens try to alter the shape of your body by tucking in your head and arms and covering the legs of your tripod with a coat or blanket.

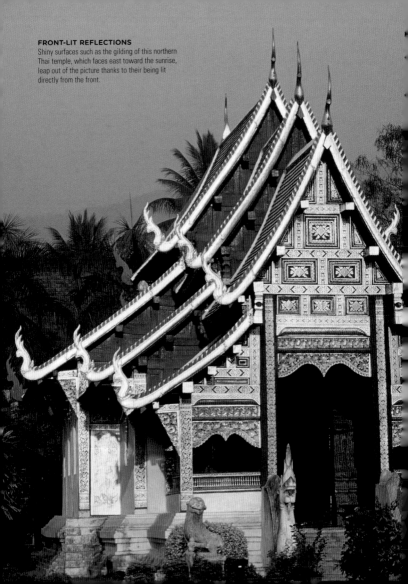

FRONT-LIT REFLECTIONS
Shiny surfaces such as the gilding of this northern
Thai temple, which faces east toward the sunrise,
leap out of the picture thanks to their being lit
directly from the front.

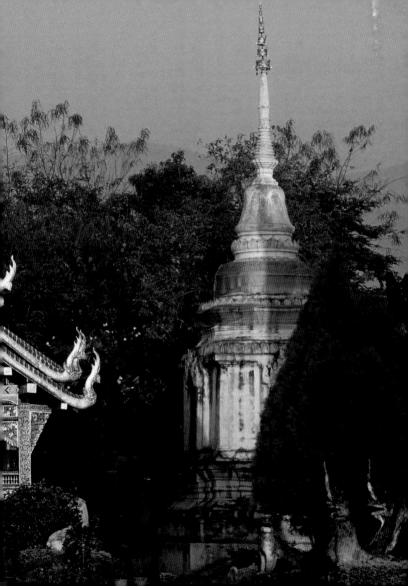

Backlighting

Perhaps the last thing an inexperienced photographer would consider is shooting directly into the sun—it just sounds counterintuitive. However, experienced photographers know that backlighting—the name given to lighting that emanates from the sun (or a reflection of the sun) directly into the camera—can produce intensely dramatic images.

The best-known example of a backlit shot is the silhouette. The key to a successful silhouette is choosing a subject that has an interesting, evocative, and easily recognizable shape, and ensuring the background is uncluttered—a clear, uniform sky is ideal. With the subject placed in front of the sun, set the camera to expose for the bright sky and not the subject. Don't expose for the sun itself or the entire image will be rendered too dark. All but the very brightest elements of the sky should show any detail (but becoming darker towards the edges of the photo), while the

subject should be a uniform black, but with a well-defined outline. Silhouettes can also be successfully captured by shooting into a reflection of the sun (off water for example) instead of the sun itself.

Undulating landscapes, or landscapes with distinctive objects set a good distance apart from one another, such as hedgerows or stands of trees, also make good back-lit images. Exposing for the sky will render the undulations or trees in silhouette, which then form horizontal layers in the final image as they recede into the distance—an effect known as "aerial perspective." This is often most successfully achieved with the sun very low in the sky, just after sunrise or just before sunset.

Another dramatic way of exploiting backlighting is to include a colorful,

A CLEAN SILHOUETTE
A simple dark-on-light, two-tone silhouette of a hawk. Here, the sun is entirely concealed by the bird.

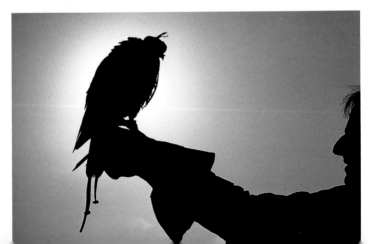

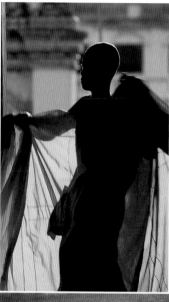

translucent object between you and the light source, such as a stained-glass window, some material, or even leaves or petals. As long as you avoid overexposure, the colors (and intricate structure, in the case of the leaf) will be brightly and delicately rendered.

One final example of backlighting involves capturing the brightly lit edges of the subject against a dark background, resulting in a phenomenon known as "edge" or "rim lighting." This slightly specialized form of backlighting is covered more fully on the next pages.

INTENSE COLOR
Backlighting through anything translucent brings out richness of color—as in the case of this monk's saffron robe—as long as you avoid overexposure. The brightly lit edges around the monk's head are a good example of rim lighting.

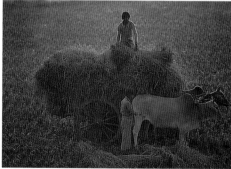

BURMA
As the dry season progresses, temperatures rise and haze increases, which gives opportunities for attractive backlighting early and late, as in this scene of farmers loading hay near Mandalay.

Rim lighting

Earlier, we looked at the various types of backlighting, and in particular the more straightforward example of the silhouette. As dramatic as silhouettes can be, they should be used sparingly in any collection of travel photos—as a photographic device they have today lost a great deal of their novelty factor. Of greater interest, to my mind at least, is the backlighting effect known as edge or rim lighting.

Rim lighting occurs when the light strikes the subject from the back but also off to one side or from higher up—this why this type of lighting is sometimes referred to as "off-axis" lighting. The resulting image will show the subject, or part of the subject, outlined in a bright highlight. The thickness and overall appearance of the rim depends on the physical characteristics of the outer layer of the subject. A smooth, hard surface, such as glass or metal, will produce a very thin, smooth rim light, while a soft, fibrous object, such as wool, will capture more light and produce a much thicker outline. Rim lighting is often used in portrait photography to outline the model's hair, and is usually most effective with a dark or fairly dark background.

Being an off-axis form of lighting, there is less contrast in a rim-lit shot than a silhouette. This is apparent when you compare the amount of color and detail visible in the subject of each type of shot—the subject of a silhouette is black and featureless, whereas that of a rim-lit shot will often show relatively good detail and a certain amount of color.

Getting the exposure right for rim lighting is complex and depends on the specific lighting conditions and the subject. The best bet is to use evaluative or matrix mode to meter the scene, then check the result and experiment with the exposure if necessary to get the effect you want.

TRANSLUCENT FISH
These dried fish are lit at their edges by the sun, which also shines through them to silhouette their bones. The camera was placed so they appeared against a background in shadow.

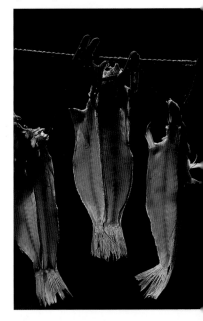

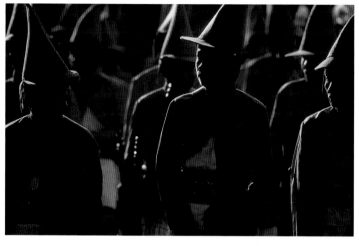

Preparation

On the road

APPRECIATING
LIGHT

87

Subjects

Themes

Reference

RIM LIGHTING
At a very low angle, almost into the picture frame,
the sun creates a rim-lighting effect. How brightly
the edges appear depends strongly on the texture
of the subject—here, cloth uniforms.

OVERALL BACKLIGHTING FLARE
The less-cearly defined edges of these waves breaking at
Point Lobos, near Carmel, California, exhibit a much looser
form of rim lighting, but the unmistakable glow is still very
much apparent.

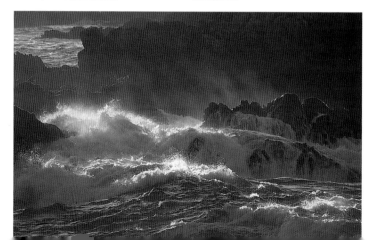

Soft light

While the position of the light source in relation to the subject or scene plays a crucial role in determining appearance, it's important to remember that the significance of the direction of the light is, itself, determined by how strong it is. Up to now we've been assuming the light is more or less direct and undiffused, such as the sun in a clear, cloudless sky—a quality often referred to as "hard" light. Here we're going to look at diffused, or "soft" light.

Naturally diffused light is the result of specific atmospheric conditions. Clouds, for example, are a principal cause of soft light—their abundance and type determining exactly how soft the light is. Thin, high-level cloud will diffuse sunlight, softening a high-contrast scene thanks to less dense and clearly defined shadow regions. A scene such as this, with a lower dynamic range between highlights and shadows, is easier to photograph without fear of over- or underexposure, while the absence of strong shadows and bright highlights can make complex shapes and scenes easier to "read." However, the continued presence of shadows, albeit in a less dominant form, still provides the desirable modeling effect for certain scenes, notably landscapes. In these softer lighting conditions colors also may appear less vibrant, but this lack of vibrancy will often make them appear more natural. For portraits, diffuse light will often be more flattering, resulting in softer features and more even skin tones.

At ground level, haze can also be helpful to the photographer as it will emphasize the distance between objects and bring a sense of depth to a long-distance view.

If the cloud cover is too heavy, on the other hand, the sunlight becomes so diffused that

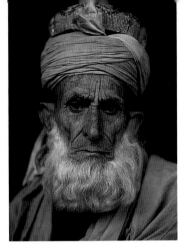

PORTRAIT LIGHTING
One of soft light's better qualities is that it does away with harsh shadows, making it useful for portraits.

clouds become nonexistent. In this case, without the modeling effect of shadows landscapes become flat and dull, objects can lose their form and texture, and all sense of light and shade is lost.

Image clarity

Soft light is good for certain subjects, particularly those with intricate shapes. One of the main characteristics of this kind of lighting is that it is clear and uncomplicated, so is good for giving distinct, legible images of complex subjects. Reflective surfaces also make for more legible images under diffuse lighting: the reflection of a broad, even light source will cover all or most of any shiny surface.

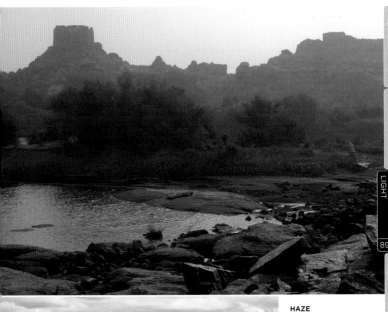

Preparation

On the road

APPRECIATING
LIGHT

89

Subjects

Themes

Reference

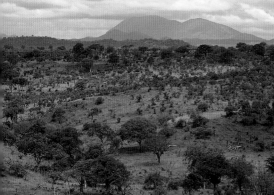

HAZE
This image of a ruined medieval stone fort overlooking the Nile in Nubia shows how haze creates aerial perspective, adding a sense of depth to a photograph.

PASTEL GREENS
Soft, shadowless light and a delicacy of color characterize landscapes under the diffuse, soft light of continuous cloud.

Daylight indoors

Not all of your time traveling and taking photos will necessarily be spent outdoors. There will undoubtedly be many occasions when you'll want to photograph the interiors of buildings or perhaps even the people who live or work there. The initial concerns about photographing indoors—primarily the lack of light and high contrast—are valid ones, so let's look at what you can hope to achieve with daylight indoors.

Shooting indoors with available light has much to recommend it—not least of all the natural quality it affords your images. However, what about low light levels? Of course, much will depend on the size and number of the windows in the room and in which direction they face. In order to get as much of the room as possible in focus (using a small aperture) you'll have to use relatively long shutter speeds—perhaps around ½ sec (at ISO 200). If you can, use a tripod or at least something sturdy on which to rest the camera, rather than increasing the ISO setting or using flash. Increasing the ISO setting may add noise to your images, while using flash is likely to upset the subtle natural lighting balance of the room and may impact on the "architecture" of the room.

Light levels fall drastically as you move further away from a window, which is why shots of interiors are usually high contrast. This is not necessarily a bad thing. Think about your composition and position the camera in such a way that it makes the most of the rise and fall in light levels.

The rapid fall-off of natural light from a window is an important consideration when photographing people indoors. They need to be very close to the window to get a sufficient amount of light to illuminate them. The most dramatic indoor portraits shot with available light are when the light source is to one side of the subject. The side of the face closest to the window will be well lit, while the other will be cast in shadow, creating a dramatic shot.

UNEXPECTED EFFECTS
When the sun is low enough to shine through a window and across a room, the light will pick out objects—though not for long, as the sun's position moves relatively quickly at these times. Here, in a Catholic church, it shone directly onto the ladder used each evening by the bell-ringer.

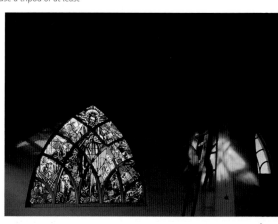

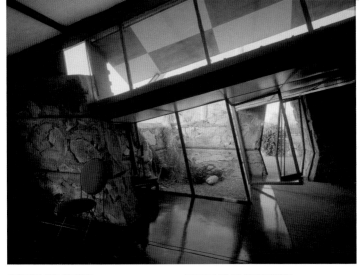

APPRECIATING
LIGHT

91

Preparation

On the road

Subjects

Themes

Reference

FRANK LLOYD WRIGHT

To avoid window highlights blowing out, choose the camera position carefully. In this room, designed by U.S. architect Frank Lloyd Wright, the viewpoint ensures that most of the sky is hidden—further back would cause too much flare, further forward would lose the shape of the awning.

THE VALUE OF REFLECTION

Bright sunlight falling on a patch of floor in front of this young novice nun illuminates the shadowed area of her face and pink robes—an effect that not only makes the details visible, but is beautiful in its own right.

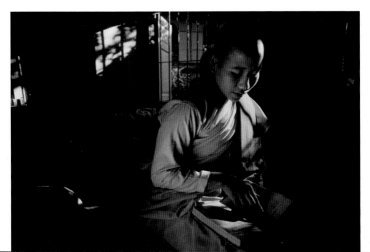

Emphasizing texture

Successfully capturing the texture of an object in a photograph can make it appear more real to the viewer. The texture reinforces the tactile nature of the object, which triggers physical memories—rough or smooth—in the viewer.

As you visit new locations with your camera, be on the lookout for artifacts and objects that reveal strong texture. More often than not you'll need to get in close to the subject to capture this texture, which may result in an abstract, nonrepresentational image. Don't worry if the viewer is unable to make out the subject in these particular photographs—as long as you have overview shots that reveal the true identity of the items—as you're trying to engage the viewer's tactile sense. Markets, woodlands, architecture (both interior and exterior)—just about everywhere you visit should be able to offer suitable subjects.

ACUTE LIGHTING ANGLE
The polished surface of this partially carved wood was brought out by light shining at an acute angle. This gives a pleasant edge to the gourd-like carved shape, and accentuates the natural grain.

As we discussed earlier in this chapter, generally the best time of day to record texture is early morning or late afternoon, when the light strikes the object at a low, raking angle. However, this does depend somewhat on the texture itself. If it is very coarse, with deep troughs and tall peaks, then the lower the angle of the light, the more the texture will be obscured by shadow.

Finally, also experiment with depth of field if you are shooting from a low angle. Selectively focusing on part of the object to reveal the texture may have greater impact than the entire frame being sharp.

Learning about texture

The best way to learn what lighting works best with which texture is to assemble a variety of objects, each of which has its own unique surface quality—a ceramic tile, some silk, bark from a tree, a metal grille, for example—it's not important as long as they exhibit strong variety between rough and smooth.

Now set up a light source, the angle of which you can easily control, such as a standard desk lamp with a bright, halogen bulb. Photograph the objects in turn at various angles, first with the bulb uncovered so that it provides direct light. Repeat the exercise but put a sheet of paper in front of the bulb to diffuse the light. Assess the images to see which combination of angle and diffuse or direct light works best with each material.

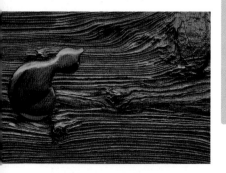

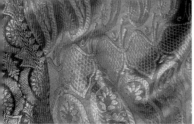

ADDING FOLDS TO TEXTILES
Textiles, and in particular silk, with its shot appearance, can easily be given character and volume simply by pushing them into folds. A moderately angled light will then bring out the varying texture.

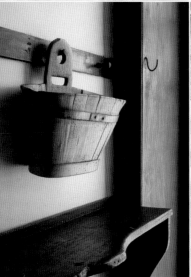

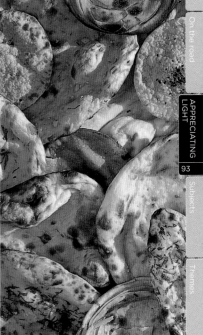

TOWARD THE WINDOW
Shooting at an oblique angle toward a large light source is one way of giving a broad highlight to rounded surfaces, in this case an old Shaker milk bucket. The light source is a north-facing window.

RAKING LIGHT
For this selection of Indian breads, a low sun was ideal. The rough, matt, appetizing texture of the breads is brought out more strongly by undiffused light.

City lights

Photographing cities at night, particularly those of foreign countries, is one of the highlights for any traveling photographer. Many cities today feature commercial centers with high-rise modern architecture, which at night can make for spectacular lighting displays. Other cities that straddle a river often feature a well-lit bridge (or even a succession of bridges), while yet more cities have large entertainment and shopping districts with acres of flashing neon signage. Images of such scenes are essential to your photo collection if you want to recreate a real sense of the excitement of traveling abroad.

As tempting as it might be simply to go exploring with your camera the first night you're there, it makes sense to find out in advance what a city has to offer with a view to nighttime photography. Look in guidebooks and on postcard stands to find out where the various districts are, what they have to offer in terms of lighting, and how to get there. Give yourself plenty of time to find a good spot from which to photograph once you arrive at your chosen destination.

The best time to shoot cities at night is actually at dusk, when there is still a little residual light left in the sky. This helps to balance the natural and artificial light sources, making the lighting less harsh than when the sky is entirely black.

As you'll be using exposures of several seconds, carry a tripod with you, or at least find something to place the camera on. You'll also need a shutter release cable (or set the camera to self-timer) and

ideally use the camera's mirror lock-up setting to stop vibration when the shutter fires. With the camera on a tripod, you can use the lowest ISO setting to avoid the risk of introducing noise to the image. In addition, use the camera's noise reduction facility if it has one. Set the camera to Aperture priority (A/Av) and begin with a setting of f/8. The camera will then work out how long the exposure needs to be. Review the results using the camera's LCD display and experiment with different aperture settings. You may find, when it gets very dark, that you'll have to use the camera's Bulb (B) setting for really long exposures.

Modern DSLR cameras, with their quick access to a wide variety of white balance settings, make photographing cities at night much more straightforward. Even using the Auto white balance setting, the mixed lighting is unlikely to result in a biased color cast—and if you're shooting in Raw you'll have no problem correcting any unwanted color cast in your shot in post-production.

KEEPING IT BRIGHT
A Shanghai street packed with seafood restaurants has a lighting level to match the buzz of nighttime business. Slightly overexposed images are often most successful.

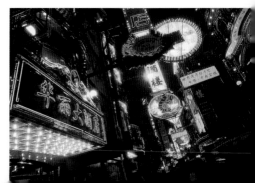

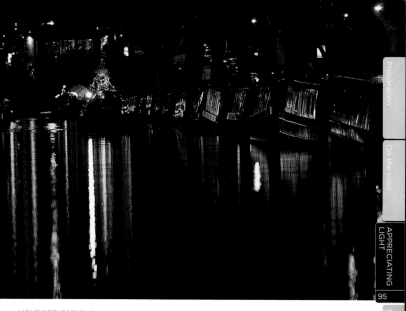

Preparation

On the road

APPRECIATING
LIGHT

95

Subjects

Themes

Reference

LIGHT REFLECTIONS

To get the most out of the fairly low lighting on a canal in London, I shot with a long telephoto at an acute angle to the moored canal boats (to catch reflections in their side panels) and from very low, for maximum reflections in the water. Without these two kinds of reflection, the shot would have been hardly readable—as it is, the effect is atmospheric and slightly mysterious.

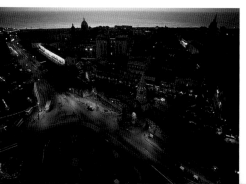

CITY AT DUSK

Twilight (just after sunset) is here an important element in an elevated view of a Caribbean city. Its muted, but general illumination helps to give definition to buildings and streets, in what would otherwise be a picture composed solely of dots and streaks of light.

Lighting displays

One of the highlights of photographing a city during the evening is capturing the brightly colored signs found in many of the entertainment districts. Fluorescent and LED lighting has, in many places, replaced neon signage as they are easier to assemble and require no potentially expensive glass-bending skills. Fluorescent lights don't have quite the same look and feel of a true neon sign, but in terms of the technique required to photograph them they are very similar.

Photographing a specific lighting display is quite different to capturing a wider cityscape view. The two major differences are, first, the best time to photograph and second, the focal lengths you need. In terms of timing, to get images of lighting displays at their best, shoot when there is no residual light left in the sky, in other words later than photographing a general cityscape. The lights tend to show up more clearly against a black sky. The second difference is an image of a specific display will have much greater impact if it fills the frame. To do this you'll need to use a telephoto lens—a telephoto zoom such as 70–200mm should give you the variety of focal lengths you'll need. Unsurprisingly, with long focal lengths it's wise to use a tripod to avoid camera shake; and even if, by zooming right into the brightly lit display, you achieve shutter speeds that allow you to hand hold the camera, the pulsating nature of fluorescent lights in particular mean that to capture the display accurately you'll need to shoot at around 1/30 sec.

In terms of metering, evaluative or matrix metering will usually work well with lighting displays. Take a shot with the metered reading and review it. Increasing the exposure will result in the display appearing thicker, but with less vibrant colors, while reducing the

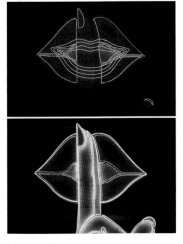

DISPLAY CYCLES
Some neon displays cycle through changes as striplights switch on and off in sequence. Try different moments in the cycle, and also vary the exposure. Neither of the exposures above is right or wrong—simply a different effect. Color is stronger with shorter exposures, but a luminous glow needs longer.

exposure will provide more vibrant colors, but the display tubes will appear thinner.

If you're lucky enough to be in a city at the time of a large celebration, you may be treated to a spectacular fireworks display. Photographing fireworks is a lot easier than you think, and can produce really breathtaking results.

Again, try to do as much planning as you can before the display begins. Consider your foregrounds and backgrounds, and make sure your view isn't going to be obscured by

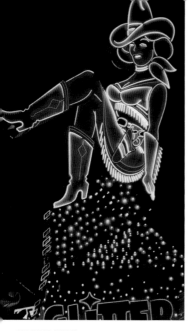

people moving in front of the camera. Set the camera on a tripod, and using a wide-angle lens or zoom setting, make sure you're framing the right part of the sky. You may need to wait for the display to begin to make sure you're pointing in the right place. Set the camera to manual, the shutter to Bulb (B), and focus to infinity. Begin with an aperture setting of around f/8, and when the first firework explodes, use a shutter release cable to hold the shutter open for as long as the firework is alight. Review the results and make any necessary alterations to the framing. Experiment with different aperture settings to see how that affects the results. Finally, be wary of which direction the wind is blowing. Fireworks produce a lot of smoke, and you don't want your images spoiled by clouds of billowing smoke obscuring parts of the display.

COLORED NEON
The green color-cast issues of shooting by fluorescent lighting are irrelevant with strongly colored displays such as this. The greenish cast remains, and you would still probably want to set the white balance accordingly, but this is largely overwhelmed by the coloring.

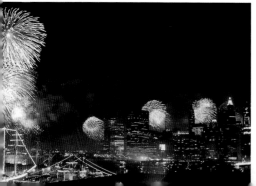

FIREWORKS
To take a wide-angle photograph of fireworks in a setting, use the start of the display to judge the height and position of the bursts, and frame the shot accordingly. With the camera locked on a tripod, vary the exposure times to include single and multiple bursts. This shot was taken in New York at the centenary celebrations of the Statue of Liberty. The lens's focal length was 35mm equivalent (slightly wider than standard), and ISO set to 100 for a noise-free image.

Preparation

On the road

APPRECIATING LIGHT

97

Subjects

Themes

Reference

Using flash

Whether built-in or as a unit attached to the camera's hot-shoe (not all cameras have this connection), on-camera flash units are designed for compactness and ease of use; with these as priorities, quality and variety of lighting take second place. However, having said that, some form of light is essential in all forms of photography, and if nothing else is available then on-camera flash at least enables the photographer to record an image, albeit often producing a somewhat unsubtle result. A typical, purely flash-lit photograph tends to feature flat illumination on the main subject and a dark background. The result is clear, sharp, and with good color separation, but is generally lacking in ambience. Typical good uses of full-on flash are close-ups of colorful subjects, as these can benefit from the crisp precision and strong colors afforded by flash illumination.

To help avoid the flat, often harsh, results of built-in flash, you really need to invest in a detachable flash unit that has a swiveling head. Fortunately, such units are relatively compact and lightweight, and so shouldn't add too much bulk to your equipment. The significance of the swiveling head is that it allows you to point the flash away from the subject, toward a pale ceiling or wall. In this way, the subject is lit from the light reflecting off a much larger surface, creating a softer illumination and less harsh shadows. This technique is known as "bounce" flash. Another alternative is to fit a translucent plastic attachment to the flash head, which will help diffuse the light from the flash, again creating a softer result. Finally, most DSLRs will allow you to adjust the output of either the built-in flash or a flash unit. While this means colors are not as vibrant, it will provide you with a less brightly lit image, which can help soften a person's features.

Another benefit of having on-camera flash is that in certain daylight situations, notably when the subject is back-lit, it can be difficult to expose for the subject without overexposing the background. Using on-camera flash to light the subject allows you to expose for both subject and background.

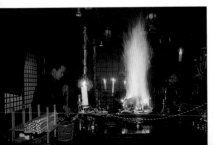

FILL FLASH
On-camera flash enables you to add to the ambient light of a scene, improving the overall exposure of an image. In this scene of fire prayers in a Japanese Buddhist monastery, the soaring flames were the key subject, but fill flash was needed to make the monk visible.

HOT-SHOE FLASH
The first step beyond your camera's built-in flash is the more flexible attachable one, which can be angled off ceilings or other surfaces, or diffused.

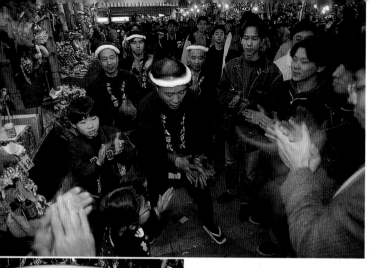

Preparation

On the road

APPRECIATING LIGHT

99

Subjects

Themes

Reference

FLASH PLUS AMBIENT
Use a slower shutter speed to capture the ambient lighting—especially with a digital SLR that allows rear-curtain flash. Used at the Tori no Ichi Festival, Tokyo.

Finally, try using on-camera flash for creative effect. With the camera set to shutter priority (or manual), select a slow shutter speed (begin with 1/15 sec). Set the camera to fire the flash. Now when you take a photo, the flash will fire, capturing part of the subject sharply, but because the shutter remains open for a fraction of a second after the flash has fired, any camera movement will result in part of the image appearing blurred. Known as slow-sync flash, some cameras can be set to fire the flash at the beginning of the exposure (front or 1st curtain sync) or at the end (rear or 2nd curtain sync).

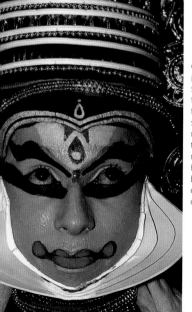

INTENSE COLOR
The great value of portable flash is that it makes it possible to take at least some kind of photograph in situations where there is insufficient light. Direct, on-camera flash pictures usually work best when the subject has strong tones and colors, as here.

SUBJECTS

Most of you will be combining a vacation with family or friends with the opportunity to photograph breathtaking scenery, a diversity of natural and manmade landmarks, perhaps new cultural experiences, and even some wildlife. This chapter covers popular holiday activities, generic destinations, and potential subjects, and provides practical advice on equipment, together with shooting tips and hints so that you'll be able to make the most of the time you spend behind the camera and return home with photographs that really capture the essence of your time away.

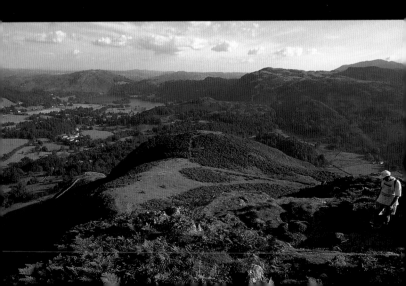

Perhaps the most important thing to remember when traveling with your camera is that, on a personal level at least, your subjects are out of the ordinary. Rather than trying to show insights into what you know best, the essence of travel photography is to get across the enthusiasm of seeing new places, people, and things. What may be unremarkable to the jaded eye of someone who sees it every day can be made into an exciting image by a photographer who comes across it for the first time. It's easy to become overfamiliar with your everyday surroundings, and forget that to a fresh eye they may be remarkable.

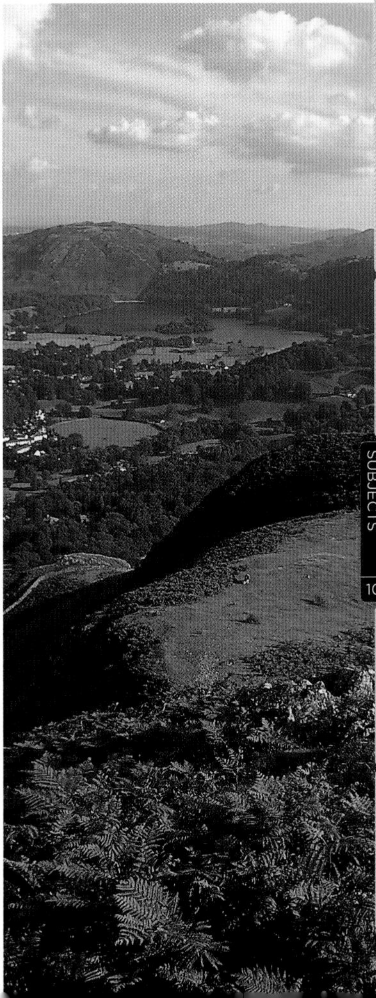

WALKING VACATIONS
Walking or trekking vacations are ideal for photography. The scenery is likely to be outstanding, and you move at a pace that allows you to savor your surroundings. This part of England's Lake District, near the town of Grasmere, is known for its spectacular rolling green hills.

Preparation

On the road

Appreciating Light

SUBJECTS

101

Themes

Reference

Wildlife

Photographing animals in the wild can result in magnificent and poignant images. Yet capturing such images requires a certain amount of skill, a good helping of luck, and a great deal of patience.

For successful wildlife photography you need to be able to fill the frame with your subject, and to do this you'll need a long focal length lens or zoom lens—an effective focal length of 500–600mm is often required. Alternatively you could consider a 2x teleconverter combined with a medium telephoto lens, such as 100–400mm. While a teleconverter will cut down on the amount of equipment you have to carry around with you, remember that you'll lose valuable light—by up to two stops—making a fast shutter speed of 1/500 sec a relatively sluggish 1/125 sec. Although you can always increase the ISO setting to get faster speeds, be wary of introducing noise to the image. Ideally, use a tripod and cable release to ensure really sharp images. If you're in a vehicle, as is often the case on many safaris for example, use a window ledge for support with a thick cloth, towel, or beanbag under the lens for support and to dampen any vibration.

Another advantage of long focal length lenses is that they have a narrow depth of field. By setting a large aperture, it is easier to blur the foreground and background, so the subject of the photo stands out in sharp focus. Aim to specifically focus on the eyes of your subject if at all possible as people automatically look for the eyes of a portrait—whether a person or an animal—and if they are slightly out of focus it detracts from the image.

If you don't have a long lens all is not lost—a wider view that shows an animal, or a group of animals, in its natural habitat can make a strong image by setting the scene and context. However, avoid the temptation to place the subject of the image in the middle of the frame, as this can emphasize the empty space around the animal. Use the rule of thirds compositional technique and place the subject off-center by about one-third from the top or bottom and from either side. As well as creating a more dynamic image, this off-centered placement also reduces the impression that the animal appears smaller than you would like.

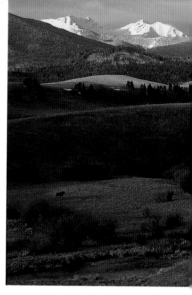

FIGURE FOR SCALE
It's still possible to capture successful wildlife images without a long telephoto lens. The small figure of a moose crossing a meadow in Montana in the spring gives action to this landscape and a sense of its vast scale.

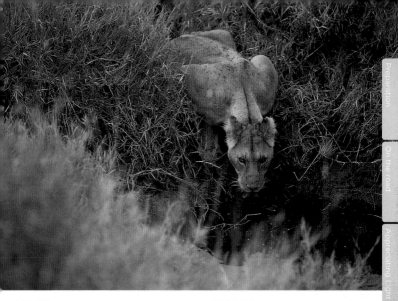

Preparation

On the road

Appreciating Light

SUBJECTS

103

Themes

Reference

LIONESS
Try to make sure that your subject's eyes are sharply in focus as these are a key element of any wildlife shot. Using a wide aperture (small f number) has also helped to blur a potentially distracting foreground.

HUNTING DOGS
This pack of hunting dogs in Tanzania's Mikumi National Park was photographed from about 65 feet (20 meters) away with a 600mm lens, from the side window of a jeep.

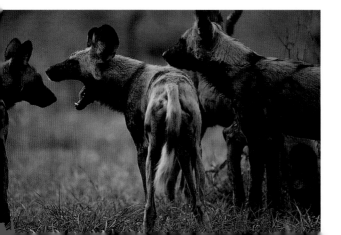

Birds

Of all wildlife subjects, birds are among the most popular subjects for photographers, and shots of birds in flight are often the most rewarding. However, photographing flying birds is not easy, and is something that requires a great deal of practice. Fortunately practicing with digital equipment is much less expensive as it is with conventional film cameras, and you have the added benefit of being able to instantly review your shots.

As with most wildlife photography, photographing birds requires a long telephoto lens so that the subject fills the frame, or at least a good portion of it. However, you may find it easier to practice tracking birds in flight with a medium telephoto lens such as a 70–200mm zoom, before moving to a focal length of 500mm or longer.

As well as filling the frame with your subject, you should also aim to use shutter speeds that are sufficiently fast to freeze all movement, that is the wing beats as well as the bird itself. Shutter speeds of 1/500 sec

IN FLIGHT
Late afternoon sunlight catches a pair of white pelicans flying against approaching stormclouds over Lake Manyara, Tanzania. Large birds such as these fly slowly, and as they were moving across the field of view, there was only a slight change in distance. Continuous automatic focusing dealt with this easily, even with a 600mm lens.

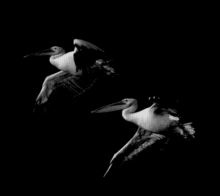

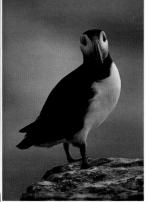

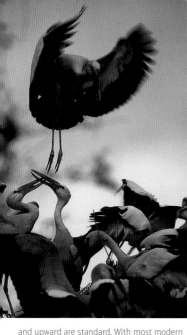

Preparation

On the road

Appreciating Light

SUBJECTS

105

Themes

Reference

PUFFIN
This single-bird, frame-filling shot of a puffin was taken on a North Sea island colony off the coast of northeastern England. Some species, such as this one, are extremely approachable, and their obvious lack of fear of humans is enhanced by the monitored and strictly restricted access to the colony.

NESTING COLONY
Seasonal nesting sites for birds that live in colonies, like these Openbill Storks, offer opportunities for great shots.

and upward are standard. With most modern digital SLRs you should be able to set the ISO sensitivity to 400 without introducing too much noise to the image, and this should help you get the required shutter speed—of course bright lighting conditions are also helpful.

Start by photographing large birds, such as herons and storks. These are ideal species to begin with as they are large and move relatively slowly. Aim to position yourself with the sun behind you and so that you are photographing the bird as it approaches. Track it using the viewfinder, and keep panning with a smooth movement even after you have taken your shots.

Utilize the camera's continuous auto focus mode if it has one. In this mode the camera will continually refocus the lens automatically while you are tracking the bird, as long as the shutter release is depressed

half way and the selected auto focus point is over the bird. With more advanced digital SLRs you can select any one of a number of points as the auto focus point, but the central point is usually the easiest for beginners (and often the fastest). Also experiment with the camera's continuous shooting, or burst, mode as this will increase the chances of capturing the shot you want. However, don't despair if your camera doesn't have these options. There are superb examples of bird-in-flight photographs taken with one-shot auto focus—it's just a matter of more practice.

As with all wildlife shots, aim to focus on the bird's eye (if you can get close enough to distinguish it!). If you're using the central focus point, this will ensure the subject is off-center and will also create "space" into which the bird can fly—two important compositional rules.

Winter scenes and sports

Snow scenes can make for powerfully evocative landscape photographs— sometimes subtly graphic as a thick blanket of white is punctuated with the dark, intriguing shapes of leafless trees, other times they dwell on the majesty of snowcapped mountains. Whatever the subject, however, if there is a large expanse of snow in the image it's essential that you consider carefully both white balance and exposure settings as your camera's metering system is likely to be tricked by the lighting conditions.

If left to its own devices a digital camera will underexpose snow scenes and produce distinctly gray-looking snow. This is because it will perceive the snow as the midtone in the image. To counter this, increase the exposure by one or two stops, either by setting the exposure compensation (EV) to between +1 and +2, or by selecting your camera's Manual (M) setting and manually increasing the exposure. Snow needs to be exposed accurately in order to capture its unique luminous quality and texture. However, be wary of overexposing as you'll lose texture in "blown" highlights. It's often a case of trial and error, so remember to review your images carefully and check the histogram for large overexposed areas.

In terms of white balance, snow will reflect the color of its surroundings, especially the blue of a clear sky. Shadows in snow on a bright sunny day are often rendered blue. Most cameras will allow you to manually adjust the white balance setting to allow for this.

Winter sports photography provides the same challenges as normal sports photography, but with the added issue of tricky exposure due to the snow. As with most sports photography you need a long focal length lens or zoom lens (500–600mm) to get close to the action. Use

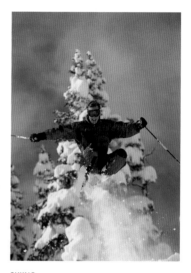

SKIING
The best moments are those where the skier is moving at speed or, as here, up in the air with the powder spraying out behind. The difficulty is in getting close enough to the action without becoming part of it. The photographer took this from a safe vantage point using a long lens with a fast shutter speed. The reflective snow and bright sun helped, giving plenty of light to work with.

the camera's continuous or predictive autofocus setting if it has one. In this mode you can track the action through the viewfinder, and while your finger is half-pressing the shutter release, the camera will continually autofocus on the subject by predicting its movement. When the subject reaches a point that makes a good composition, fully depress the shutter release and the camera will take the photo—and with

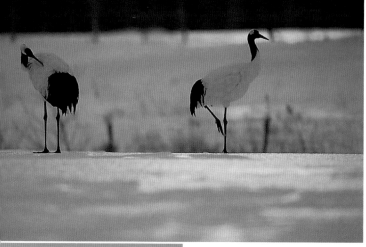

Preparation

On the road

Appreciating Light

SUBJECTS

107

Themes

Reference

CRANES
Japanese cranes at the crane sanctuary near Tsurui. Like many snow-dwellers, the cranes have partly white plumage. This makes exposure critical, both to keep the white white, without blowing out, and to separate the plumage from snow.

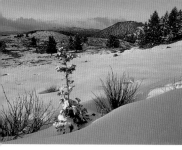

FRESH SNOW
As with sand dunes, you need to plan your view of fresh snowdrifts a little in advance, particularly if you are using a wide-angle lens from close to capture foreground detail. Footprints usually spoil shots like this when they are visible.

a sufficiently fast shutter speed, the subject will be sharply in focus. Fast shutter speeds are essential for any sports photography, anything less than 1/250 sec is likely to result in a blurred image; and if you're using a long lens, you'll want to use such speeds to avoid camera shake.

Although most of the time you're trying to freeze the action with a fast shutter speed, now and again experiment with slower speeds to capture an image with creative blur. This can add a sense of movement to the photo.

Alternatively try panning as you take the shot so that while the subject is captured in focus the background is blurred, again creating a sense of movement.

Effective sports shots can be achieved with wide-angle lenses, but it's important to get as close to the action as possible. Knowing where the best action will occur is paramount. Position yourself as close as possible without running the risk of endangering either yourself or the person you're photographing.

City break

A city break is an excellent way to get away from your normal routine, enjoy new sights, perhaps experience a different culture, and get some great images. Planning a walking route (or series of routes) is one of the most effective ways of covering the important locations, and to save time research these in advance. Most city breaks give you three or four days to explore, and within that time you should be able to see the main sights, as well as having a relaxing break, which may be paramount for your traveling companion!

Set aside day one for familiarization, getting accustomed to the city, and relaxing. Whatever the preparations and research, every photographer has a different eye for things, and nothing beats an on-the-ground assessment of the most effective viewpoint

108

Mapping the schedule

A marked-up street map shows the plan for part of one day in central London. The aims are specific—in this case including details of traditional signs and shops around Piccadilly, and a formal photograph of County Hall. The timing is keyed by the daily Changing of the Guard and by sunset.

and its timing. Sunlight, weather, and the daily round of activity all help determine the best time for shooting, which can be left to the days ahead.

Cities have such a concentration of activity and sights—all of it easy to research—that they benefit from a plan of action. How detailed the planning is depends on the type of person you are and how much time you want to devote to photography. One approach is to simply photograph the sights you see as you come across them. The opposite approach is a self-assigned shot list, in which case the plan will aim to cover every location with economy of time while paying attention to the light and timing of certain events. In the example here, one day of a trip to the heart of London, the Changing of the Guard at Buckingham Palace takes place at precisely 11:30 in the morning, and much of the rest of the day hinges on this. It is important to allow room for the unexpected, so a plan such as the one shown here is divided into zones, and the idea is to wander around the back streets as well as the main roads, alert for whatever may happen. And if something of special interest turns up, the entire plan may simply be jettisoned.

City lights

For a night-time shot, consider the floodlighting and window lights. Cities are more brightly lit after sunset than before sunrise, and more so in winter than summer. Different types of light—street lighting, neon displays, and building floodlights—are switched on at different times. Few people locally know these times, although for a specific building staff may be able to tell you. Otherwise, make a recce the evening before. Timing is important as the best time is usually dusk, when there is still sufficient natural light to reveal the building's outline.

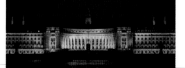

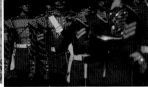

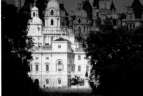

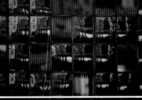

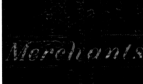

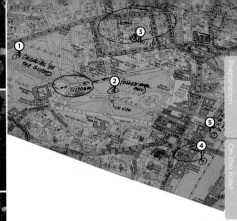

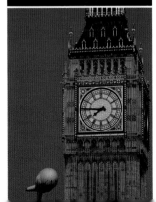

Preparation

On the road

Appreciating Light

SUBJECTS

109

Themes

Reference

1. CHANGING OF THE GUARD
Weather permitting, this takes place at 11:30am, and the short route is always the same. The viewpoint has been chosen in advance, and because the event attracts crowds of tourists, plan to be in position at least half an hour beforehand.

2. WHITEHALL FROM THE PARK
St. James's Park is the oldest of London's several royal parks, founded by Henry VIII, and is definitely worth photographing. It is also a convenient location for when the Changing of the Guard has finished. There are classic views of Whitehall and Horse Guards' Parade.

3. LONDON BUS
Piccadilly is just ten minutes' walk north of St. James's Park. The photographer had in mind an alternate approach—concentrating on details. Here, the bottle-glass of an old window offered repeated, distorted reflections, and a different take on the red double-decker bus, one of London's symbols.

4. WINE MERCHANTS
The small streets around Piccadilly are crammed with traditional shops, some dating back two centuries and more. The plan was to hunt out obscure details, such as this hand-painted gilded lettering on a door that has been endlessly repainted.

5. BIG BEN
Some city sights are so well-known as to offer almost nothing new to the photographer. Nevertheless, they may simply have to be done—in this case, Big Ben, probably the most recognizable part of the famous Houses of Parliament. Fortunately, it had two things going for it on this day—good weather, and a tethered blimp, which at least added something unusual.

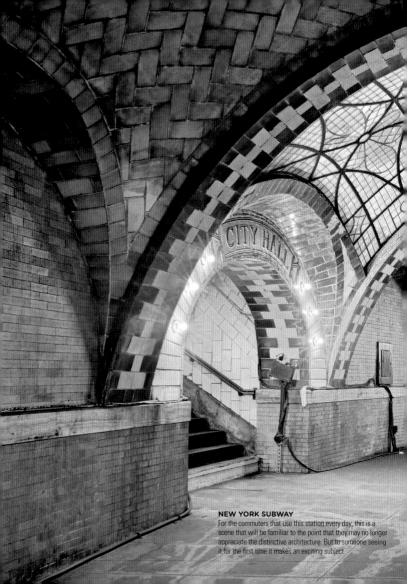

NEW YORK SUBWAY

For the commuters that use this station every day, this is a scene that will be familiar to the point that they may no longer appreciate the distinctive architecture. But to someone seeing it for the first time it makes an exciting subject.

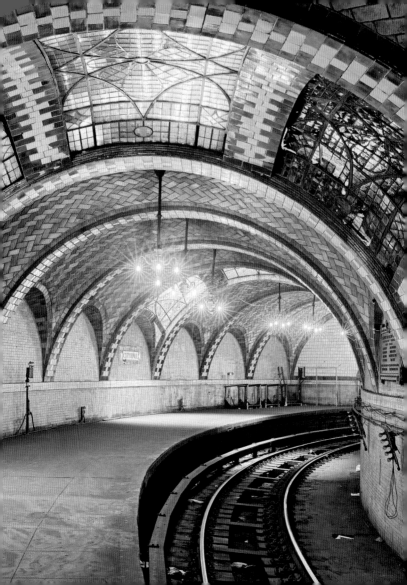

Mountain trekking

As well as being an exhilarating experience in its own right, mountain trekking is also really the only way of getting a true sense of mountain landscapes. While roadside lookouts can offer good views, only trekking gives the opportunity for in-depth coverage. As this means carrying everything you need, weight and bulk are issues; packing needs careful consideration.

In the trekking example shown here—across the trans-Himalaya from northwestern Nepal into western Tibet and around Mount Kailash—the camping gear was carried by Sherpas and yaks. One unavoidable problem is that whatever equipment is in the backpack takes time to unload. This slows down the photography, but is a better option than carrying the camera loose and risking an accident. Some backpacks are designed to rotate easily from back to front, giving you relatively quick access to your equipment.

Mountain areas vary in their picture possibilities, and it is important to cover all aspects. Dramatic landscapes figure strongly, and these depend mainly on two things—viewpoint and light. Mountain weather can be variable, so be prepared for a change in the light; early mornings and late afternoons are, as anywhere, often very good. This trek, however, offered much more in cultural material, as pilgrims from all over Tibet converge on the sacred mountain Kailash to circumnambulate it.

VERTICAL FRAMING
Mountains and hill country afford good opportunities for framing vertical shots. There are often plenty of foregrounds to choose from, particularly when taking downward-looking shots.

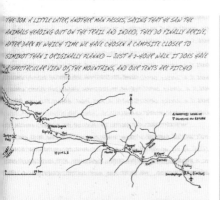

TREKKING: WEEK ONE
Planning a route in advance is the best way of ensuring you get to all the places you want to see.

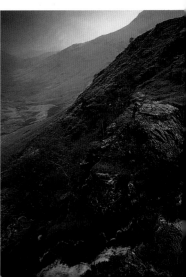

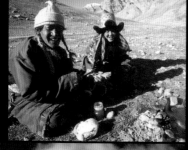

PILGRIMS
Language is not a barrier under these circumstances, as everyone is in a cheerful mood. For this shot of a couple brewing yak-butter tea, the photographer sat down and made attempts at sign language.

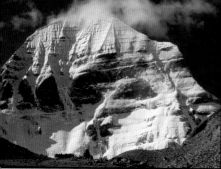

THIN AIR
With half the density of atmosphere as at sea level, views at 16,500 feet (5,000 m) are stunningly clear, even with a telephoto lens, as shown in this shot of the north face of Mount Kailash in western Tibet.

MOUNTAIN LIGHT
Lighting effects are unpredictable, but it is worth getting up before dawn for whatever the light offers—in this case a view down the Karnali Valley toward Kanjirobe. This shot calls for a long telephoto; review the shot on the LCD monitor.

Preparation

On the road

Appreciating Light

SUBJECTS

113

Themes

Reference

Walking

Although perhaps less exotic and adventurous, and certainly less arduous, than trekking in the mountains, walking can still provide the photographer with ample scope for wonderful images. Although not a vacation, the benefits of walking locally are numerous. If you have intimate knowledge of your surrounding area you'll know how it responds and reacts to different lighting conditions—whether sunny or overcast, early in the day or late afternoon, summer or winter. Using this knowledge and the variation in the conditions is an excellent way to explore, expand, and improve your own photographic eye. There may be one particular spot which, while on a bright summer's morning provides a rich palette of color, is entirely transformed in winter, but is still a striking photographic subject—the warm colors and tones replaced by a stark, graphic landscape that is the ideal subject for a black and white composition.

The changing seasons force the photographer to think about the basic tools of landscape composition—leading lines, shapes, color, tone, viewpoint, foreground, framing, and so on, and walking allows for a close and intimate examination of the countryside and exploration of these tools, all in a timely manner that is often not possible during an itinerary-packed vacation.

While it is natural to think of the changing seasons as relating specifically to the countryside, similar explorations of composition and technique are equally possible when walking around an urban environment.

Another benefit of walking locally is that you're safe in the knowledge that you can return to the same place under the same or similar lighting conditions at some point in the future—this is not a once in a lifetime journey never to be repeated, forcing you to attempt to capture the scenes before you as quickly as possible. For this reason you can experiment with your technique and take with you, for example, only a 50mm lens, or set yourself the assignment of shooting only patterns or textures. Not only will this help you to improve as a photographer by forcing you to look afresh at familiar scenes, but it has the added benefit of allowing you to carry less equipment, making the whole experience a great deal more comfortable.

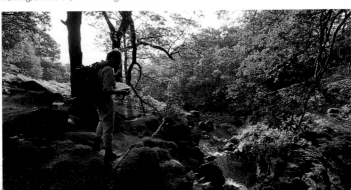

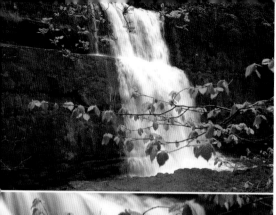

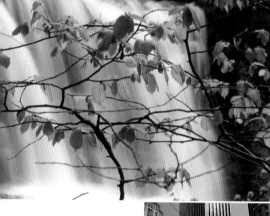

EXPERIMENT

Walking usually gives your mind time to consider your options more fully. The subject here is a forest waterfall. This was attractive enough in a long shot, but not particularly distinctive. Using a longer focal length, it was possible to fill the frame with falling water, but keeping the focus on the leaves in the foreground. A long exposure turned the water into a streaked blur, but it is still very much the subject of the shot.

EYE FOR DETAIL

Walking in order to immerse yourself in your surroundings isn't reserved for those who live in the country. Towns and cities are equally valid places in which to nurture your creativity. Here, the bright new texture of a parked van picked up street colors in downtown San Francisco.

Preparation

On the road

Appreciating Light

SUBJECTS

115

Themes

Reference

Diving

Capturing successful underwater photographs is easier now than it ever has been. Today there is a wide range of submersible housings for just about all makes of digital camera, from the fairly inexpensive models designed for compact cameras to more sophisticated (and expensive) ones that can safely house a digital SLR while still providing access to all the camera's controls.

Before embarking on photographing underwater, however, it is essential that you gain all the necessary diving qualifications. Even if you're snorkeling it's important to get fully trained by a qualified instructor. The oceans can be very dangerous, and the best places to take photographs, such as coral reefs, are often the most dangerous of all.

In purely photographic terms, the greatest problem to overcome is the absorbtion of light and color; and the deeper you go, the darker and bluer it becomes. If you're shooting with available light, one of the best ways to ensure your images retain accurate color is to shoot a diver's white slate to customize your camera's white balance setting. In addition, shoot in Raw. Raw files allow for much greater color adjustment during postproduction than JPEGs.

Although it's possible to take underwater photographs using available light, the results are likely to lack color saturation and contrast, even if shot only a few feet down in clear water on a sunny day; and if you're any deeper there simply won't be enough light to photograph at all. The only effective way to overcome this is to use flash (or when referring to underwater flash, a strobe). The strobe is usually mounted on an arm above and to one side of the camera to help avoid "back-scattering," where water particles

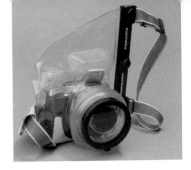

FLEXIBLE CASE
This sealed plastic container is flexible enough to allow use of the camera, with a special clear lenspiece, but sturdy enough to make it waterproof.

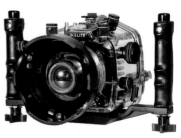

DIGITAL SLR
Underwater housings for digital SLRs, such as this one from Ikelite, provide easy access to all the camera's controls, giving the photographer full creative control.

RIGID CASE
Some manufacturers market rigid waterproof housings which, like this one from Sony, allows the use of a camera and its controls underwater, via special buttons.

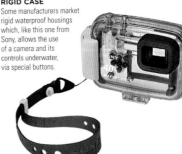

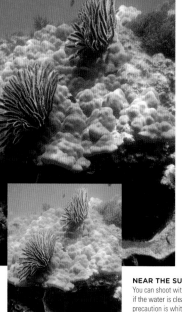

Preparation

On the road

Appreciating Light

SUBJECTS

117

Themes

Reference

Underwater shooting tips

- Vary the shutter speed—some subjects, such as fast-moving fish are often most effectively captured using a slower shutter speed that introduces some creative blur.
- Get close to your subject, not only to fill the frame, but also to minimize the amount of water between the camera and the subject.
- Shoot your subject from below if possible. This helps to isolate it from potentially distracting backgrounds.
- Concentrate on one particular form of underwater photography, such as close-ups or scenics. Take time to master the skills for each specific type before moving onto another form. Avoid the temptation to shoot everything you see.

NEAR THE SURFACE
You can shoot without flash within a few feet of the surface, if the water is clear and the sunshine bright. The main precaution is white balance. This pair of images shows the difference between the blue cast of an uncorrected shot (inset) and the more natural tones of the corrected shot (main image).

between the camera and the subject are lit up and resemble falling snow.

Remember also that water acts like an additional lens between your camera and the subject. Objects appear closer by a quarter of their distance and around a third larger than their true size. If you're using a wide-angle lens (efl 20-35mm is recomended) use a domed port in the housing. A dome port will correct the refraction issues already mentioned and also correct the problems of distortion and poor resolution close to the edges of the picture. If, however, you intend to shoot close-ups with a long focal length, use a flat port.

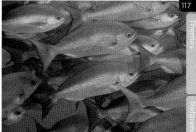

UNDERWATER SCALE
Water acts like a lens, so objects appear closer to the camera, and larger, making it easier to fill the frame.

Deserts

Deserts are defined by their lack of water. In such dry conditions, the landscape can be highly photogenic, and certainly unusual, because there is so little vegetation. The scenery is bare and rugged, with all the geology exposed. All of this makes them wonderful sources of graphic imagery, made all the more dramatic by the clear sunlight that prevails.

Desert landscape varies in type more than most people expect, and it is certainly not all sanddunes. Desert pavement—known as *reg* in the Sahara—is a surface of rocks and gravel scoured by the wind, and is among the most common. Rocky uplands usually stand out abruptly from the generally level desert terrain, and are often sharp and angular from wind weathering and runoff erosion from the infrequent but powerful rains—in some areas, such as northern Arizona, these can take the form of dangerous flash floods. Dunes are less common, but once they have started to form they are self-perpetuating and very photogenic. What little vegetation there is tends to be in the form of scrub and grasses, and the latter in particular are very distinctive and make strong shapes.

The light in deserts is usually strong and bright, with well-defined sunrises and sunsets. Nights are often clear, giving some opportunities for shooting by moonlight. The relief and texture of sand dunes and rocks looks at its most dramatic in strong, low sunlight, and this is fairly reliable. Shadows take on special importance for photography. Even in the middle of the day there is an ethereal, hard kind of beauty. In canyons between high, close rock faces, the light can bounce around, tinged by the (usually) warm colors of the stone and the blue skylight. Circular polarizing filters in clear light have a very noticeable effect.

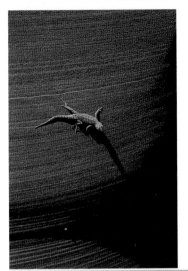

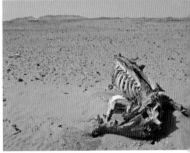

SANDSTONE WALLS
Cross-lighting reveals the fine details of texture on the water-eroded red sandstone wall of a slot canyon in Arizona, near Lake Powell, as a small lizard crosses it.

CAMEL ROUTE
The camel routes across this inhospitable desert in Africa are dotted with the skeletons of camels that die of thirst and exhaustion.

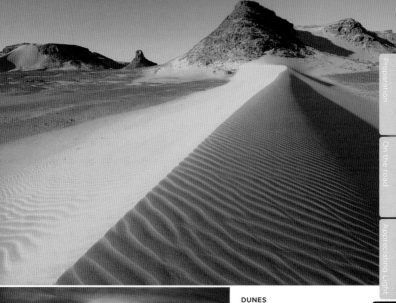

Preparation

On the road

Appreciating Light

SUBJECTS

119

Themes

Reference

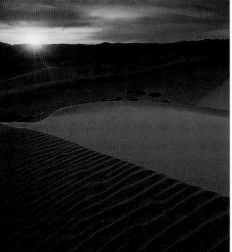

DUNES
A classic ridge dune tailing away from a rocky outcrop in northern Sudan. The angle of the light is important for revealing ripples and the granular texture.

DEATH VALLEY
Desert dunes are highly sculptural, and have different appearances during the day according ot the light. A low sun shows up the ripples on one face of a dune in Death Valley, California. You need to plan your approach carefully to avoid photographing your own unsightly footprints.

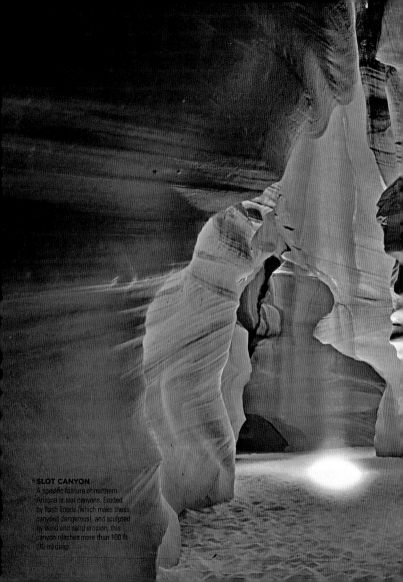

SLOT CANYON
A specific feature of northern Arizona is slot canyons. Eroded by flash floods (which make these canyons dangerous), and sculpted by wind and sand erosion, this canyon reaches more than 100 ft (30 m) deep.

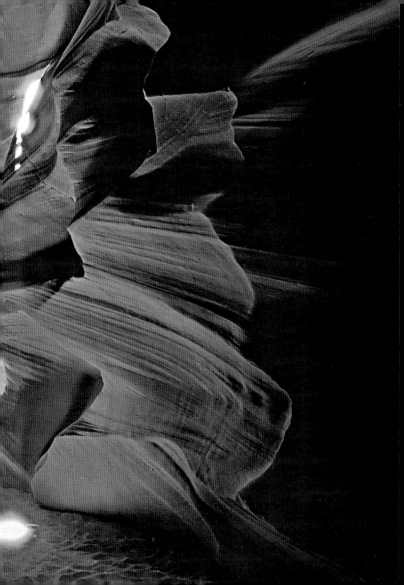

Cycling

A quick search on the Internet will reveal just how popular cycling vacations have become in recent years. There is a vast selection of well-organized and established tours in many parts of the world, catering for all ages and abilities, many are intended to take you to areas of outstanding natural beauty, making cycling vacations an ideal opportunity to photograph some breathtaking scenery. It's worth checking with the tour operator, however, to let them know that you intend to take lots of photos. Some tours are geared up for fairly fast mountain biking, and your co-riders may not be as keen to stop as often as you!

In many ways, cycling offers the photographer the best of both worlds. On the one hand, you'll cover greater distances on a bicycle than you would if walking, and you're therefore more likely to see (and have access to photograph) a greater variety of scenes. At the same time, you have the option of stopping whenever and wherever you want if something suddenly catches your eye, which is simply not possible if driving on a busy coastal road, for example.

The equipment you'll need for a cycling tour is very much dependent on what you intend to do with your images. A compact

PLANNING IS THE KEY
Before you embark on your tour, find out as much as you can about the sort of terrain you'll be covering. You don't want to carry too much on your back if you'll be using difficult mountain routes. Ideally you want to stick to green lanes and country roads.

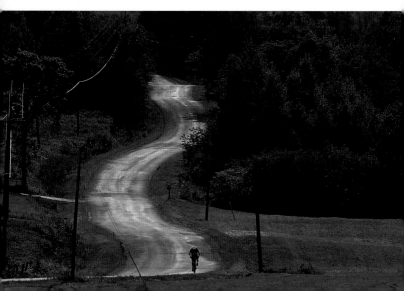

camera will be suitable for vacation snaps and family photos, and many now have "superzoom" lenses covering effective focal lengths of 30–500mm or more. Certainly a lightweight option, but if you're planning to sell your images to a stock agency, for example, you'll need more substantial equipment.

The most versatile setup (while still providing excellent image quality) is a digital SLR camera body and two zoom lenses, with typical effective focal lengths of around 25–100mm and 100–400mm. This would cover almost all the focal lengths you'll need, from wide angle for landscapes to telephoto for wildlife. You could also consider including a 2x teleconverter, which would double the long focal length without taking up too much valuable storage space.

If traveling light is a priority, you might consider taking one zoom that covers effective focal lengths of around 25-300mm. However, any zoom with a magnification of x12 is likely to be compromised slightly in terms of image quality.

Whatever equipment you decide on, be sure to include a sufficient number of memory cards for the length of your trip, a spare battery or two, and a battery charger (with adapters if you're traveling abroad).

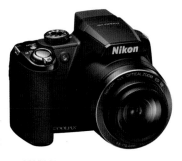

SUPERZOOM
One of the latest examples of a fixed lens "superzoom," this particular model from Nikon features a staggering 24x optical zoom with an effective focal length range of 26–624mm.

LONG ZOOM
Many lens manufacturers now produce long zooms, such as this one from Canon, which on a cropped digital SLR has an effective focal length zoom of 27–300mm. This will cover most shooting opportunities and help keep your camera equipment to a minimum.

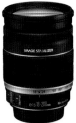

ON THE ROAD
Cycling tours can take you to some of the most beautiful scenery in the world, such as the romantic, yet spectacular, region of Tuscany in Italy.

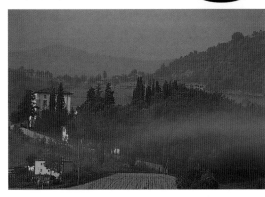

Preparation

On the road

Appreciating Light

SUBJECTS

123

Themes

Reference

On the beach

Tourism is a major international industry, and has a big impact on travel and travel destinations. Many of the most attractive locations, particularly if they are by the sea, are dedicated to vacations and leisure. They are an inescapable feature of modern traveling, although whether photographers find them a blemish or a picture opportunity depends on the motives for their own trip. If a vacation is your main purpose for travel, with photography as an extra, then you will probably be better disposed toward beaches, resorts, and the like, than if you are looking for the traditional ways of life in your chosen destination. Certainly, tourist resorts are usually far from the cultural life of their host countries, even though they may play a significant part in the economy.

In fact, these pockets of tourism have their own unique culture, and sometimes landscape, even if it may occasionally seem crass and vulgar. Treat them as another facet of travel and they can make worthwhile subjects. I should add that well-executed photography of beautiful resorts, performed without any sense of irony, is eminently commercial. There is a constant demand in the world of stock photography for images that celebrate the desirability of these destinations.

Beachscapes are a challenge for photography because their real appeal lies as much in beach culture and relaxation as in visual beauty. In fact, a flat beach of sand strewn with bodies usually needs some help to turn it into an attractive photograph. One classic solution is to step right back, even as far as a headland, and use a long focal length to compress the various elements of the view: sand, palm trees, rocks, waves. At the same

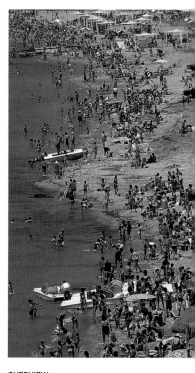

OVERVIEW
A long establishing shot of a Greek beach taken from a neighboring headland.

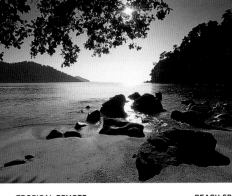

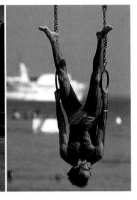

Preparation

On the road

Appreciating Light

SUBJECTS

125

Themes

Reference

TROPICAL REMOTE
Late afternoon on an island in the Andaman Sea,
capturing the essence of unspoiled nature.

BEACH SPORTS
Tourist beaches are prime sites for observing people
displaying themselves in all kinds of ways.

time, this approach tends to hide litter and
other unsightly details. An alternative is the
minimal: the deserted, away-from-it-all,
dream beach. Here, the generally accepted
ideal ingredients are a simple arrangement
of deep blue sky, blue-green sea, white sand,
and an elegantly shaped coconut palm. By
definition these are hard to find, although the
time of day may help. Early mornings have
much to recommend them, with few (if any)
tourists and the possibility that the tide has
cleaned part of the beach of litter and
footprints. The light at sunrise is also likely
to be a plus.

Beaches and resorts do, on the whole,
deserve to be seen in good weather and
attractive light, and this is how most people
like to think of them. That indeed is why they
are seasonal locations, so if you are there
during high season you will know what to
expect. That said, photography is largely
about surprises, and unusual lighting can
work wonders.

On the water

There's much to recommend taking a camera with you if you're going on a boating vacation, despite the proximity to vast amounts of water. Of course, this does depend somewhat on the nature of the vacation. If the intention is to push yourself on a grueling ocean crossing where the sailing is paramount, then you're unlikely to get much opportunity for photography (and there would be little to photograph anyway). If, however, the intention is to island-hop around the Thousand Islands, the Carribean, or the Aegean, then you'll find plenty to photograph.

The best reason to sail or cruise inshore, hugging the coastline, is that you have access to places that are inaccessible by car or even on foot. You'll stumble across coves and beaches deserted of people—ideal subjects for romantic images. In fact wherever the sea meets the land there are usually excellent photographic opportunities.

It's likely that in such locations light levels will be high, made even higher by the reflections from the sea, surf, and sand. For this reason, don't rely too heavily on automatic exposure, as the reflected light may render everything other than the sea in the image too dark. Check the histogram for exposure levels and adjust as necessary.

One essential piece of equipment when photographing coastlines is a UV (ultraviolet) filter. This will not only cut down on the

POINT LOBOS
Shooting from a boat toward the shore, into the sun when it is low, allows you to capture graphic shots of backlit waves and spray against dark rocks.

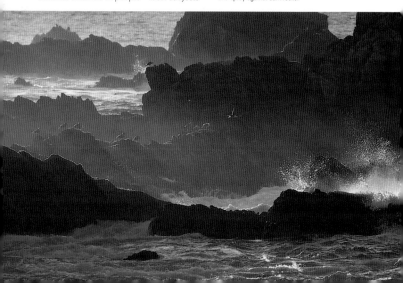

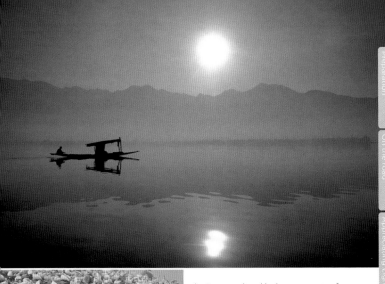

Preparation

On the road

Appreciating Light

SUBJECTS

127

Themes

Reference

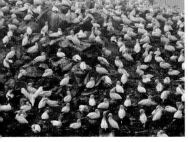

PARADISE
Often the only way to access and to photograph unspoilt paradise is by sea. In these conditions it's worth under-exposing slightly as it accentuates the colors in both the sky and the water.

BIRD COLONY
Some colonies of seabirds can only be photographed from the sea, and for this reason it's worth taking a long telephoto lens with you on any boating vacation to get optically closer to shore.

haziness produced by large amounts of ultraviolet light from the sun and reflected off the water, but it will also help to protect the front element of the lens if it is sufficiently windy enough to throw up spray. You should also consider taking a polarizing filter. As well as accentuating blue skies and white clouds, a polarizing filter will help to reduce unwanted reflections off crystal clear water, which may help you to capture some underwater details.

If waves are large and spectacular against a rocky coastline, shooting into the sun will provide backlit spray and bright reflections against dark rocks.

Rocky coasts in particular are home to numerous species of birds, and photographing their colonies from the sea is often the only way to capture them. For this you'll need a long telephoto or zoom lens, at least an equivalent focal length of around 400–500mm. Use this lens also to isolate out interesting coastal features for graphic images.

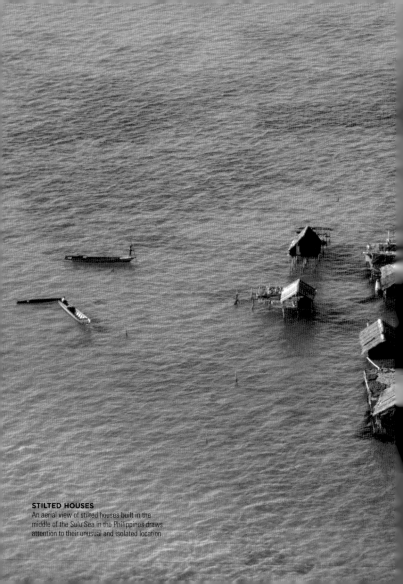

STILTED HOUSES
An aerial view of stilted houses built in the middle of the Sulu Sea in the Philippines draws attention to their unusual and isolated location.

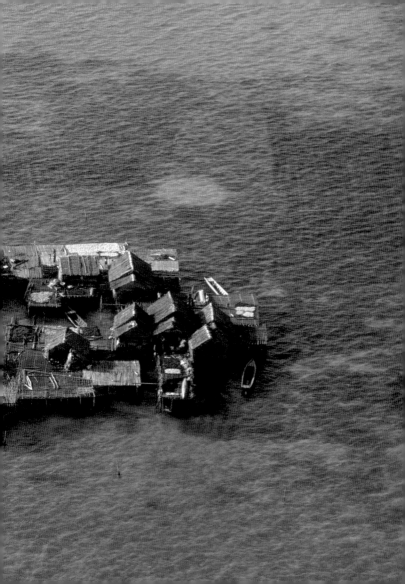

THEMES

While traveling with a camera positively encourages us to photograph a wide variety of subjects—from landscapes and wildlife to busy cities and their own unique landmarks, at the same time, a collection of travel photographs will nearly always benefit if the images share a common theme, so creating a sense of continuity. Over the following pages we'll explore the idea of themes—how to go about finding one and how to capture it successfully with your camera. Each time you travel to a new destination you can pick up on previously explored themes and add to your collection.

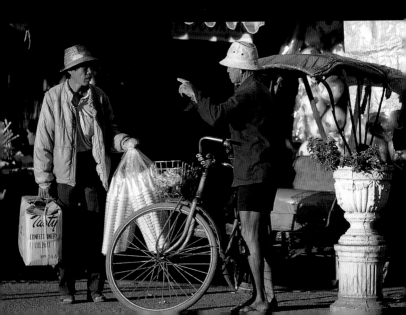

Many photographers naturally develop an identifiable style—some more definite than others—and this tends to give continuity. Style, however, is not easy to play with and manipulate. Deliberate attempts to change it or add to it can often end up looking mannered or gimmicky. A more plausible way of bringing continuity to the photographic record of a trip is to focus on one or more themes. Typically, these revolve around subject matter.

A particular destination may suggest its own storyline very easily, such as a Thai country town, as in the example here— immediately striking are the distinctive Buddhist temples, monks, cycle rickshaws, and graphics. Of course, these are the things that catch a Westerner's eye—for a Thai they are normal and less immediately interesting. Another theme might be the journey itself— or one aspect of it. As we shall see later in the chapter, on an Aegean cruise on a newly built four-masted clipper ship, the work of the crew had a special interest. Large sailing ships are not so common, and the skills for dealing with the sails and rigging are now rare.

Preparation

On the road

Appreciating Light

Subjects

THEMES

131

Reference

CYCLE RICKSHAW
It is usually your specific destination that will suggest a theme that you can work into your photography. Introducing a theme will help to create a series of images that have continuity, so adding impact to the collection.

Finding a theme

Themes may suggest themselves as you travel around a region, simply by catching your eye. The Indian street graphics shown here are just such an example. But perhaps the most fruitful way of finding a theme is to follow your personal interests and whims. These could be in art, architecture, transportation, food, children's toys, and games, anything.

I have a friend who is crazy about photographing reptiles, and over the years this has given him a very purposeful itinerary, as well as an outstanding collection of images. A more casual idea is the collection of hands at work, a few of which are shown here. This kind of shot crops up regularly in magzines and for that reason they make good stock photos Not all are interesting, but some are quite unusual, and when assembled together, they tend to enhance each other. The viewer makes connections and comparisons. Themes like these give direction and purpose to travel, even when they are just occasional asides.

INDIAN GRAPHICS
Two of the characteristics of popular graphics in India are the vibrant use of color and painting by hand. Painted signs are idiosyncratic rather than slick, and the subject makes a rewarding theme.

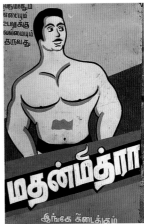

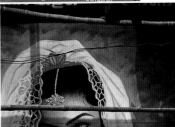

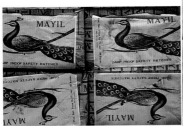

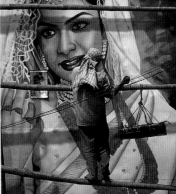

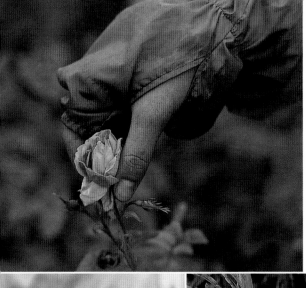

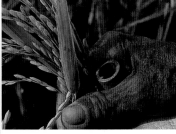

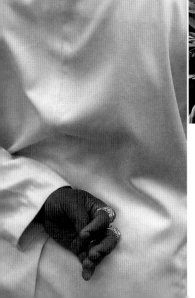

HANDS

Three of a large collection of close-ups taken in many different situations and countries, wherever there are hands doing something unusual or interesting. At top, a Bulgarian girl picks roses for perfume, above a Javanese farmer harvests rice stalks one by one, and left a Balinese priest at a temple ceremony.

Preparation

On the road

Appreciating Light

Subjects

THEMES

133

Reference

The journey

There is a fundamental difference in approach between traveling to and traveling through. Time is a luxury that very few of us have as much of as we would like, and for the majority of people embarking on a trip, the idea is usually to get to the destination as quickly and painlessly as possible. This normally means by plane, and air travel is now one of the cheapest means. It is also typically organized, bland, and unexceptional. Add to this the strict security operating on aircraft and at airports and you have little incentive to include this part of the journey in your photography.

Which is a pity, because the process of travel is itself full of potential for experience, incident, and photography. There are, for example, the views en route. Carl Mydans, a veteran Life magazine photographer from the earliest days, thought that trains provided "excellent opportunities" because they "usually ride higher than the areas they pass through and the view from them is often commanding, surpassing what can be photographed from ground level." Other means of transportation offer other, different windows on the land. Canals, for example, having been built for an older era in most countries, cut through countryside and urban areas against the grain of modern networks of road and rail. As Mydans put it, such transportation systems give "chances to … photograph the backyards—the underside of a country's life that might be missed traveling by plane."

More than this, the journey may provide you with a behind-the-scenes look at the transportation system you are using. Trains, boats, and coaches each have their own lore, and are generally not as restricted of access to photography as are aircraft (this varies from country to country). Even if you do arrive at your general destination by air, you are likely to be traveling on by different means within the country or region. Take the opportunity to discover what is special about the vehicles you use, and their drivers.

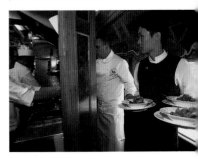

ORIENT EXPRESS
Run by the same company that owns the original, and still-running, Orient Express in Europe, this narrow-gauge train operates largely for tourists between Singapore and Bangkok. Life and activity on board makes a feature story for an American magazine, including Thai classical dance performance in the swaying dining car and the cramped but highly efficient galley operation at meal times.

AMBASSADOR
The Ambassador car, unchanged since the 1950s, is so much a part of India's heritage that it is a worthy subject of photography on its own merits. This luxury model is part of a fleet belonging to a five-star hotel in Agra.

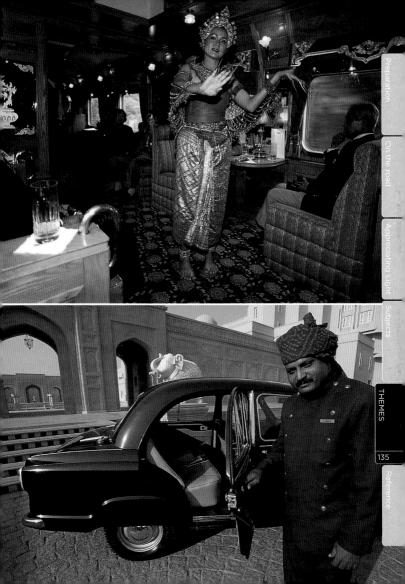

Preparation

On the road

Appreciating Light

Subjects

THEMES

135

Reference

Travel

Developing the theme introduced on the previous pages—of the journey as a subject worthy of becoming a part of the overall photography—there are some circumstances in which travel, more than destination, can be made the subject. One such occasion is a cruise, and in particular the cruise shown here, in the eastern Mediterranean on a four-masted schooner, newly built but to a traditional design. Unlike normal cruise liners this vessel, Star Flyer, carried only a hundred passengers and did so mainly under sail. Inevitably, despite the obvious attractions of the Greek island ports of call, such as Mykonos and Patmos, the workings of a sailing ship caught the attention of everyone on board. For some passengers, this was by far the main attraction. Technically interesting and supremely photogenic, the ship itself was the star of the week's cruise.

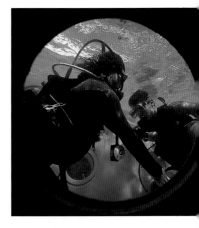

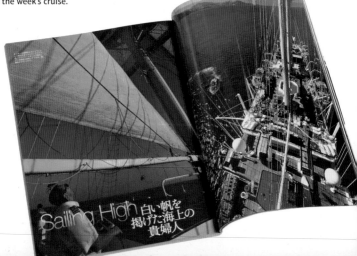

Sailing High 白い帆を掲げた海上の貴婦人

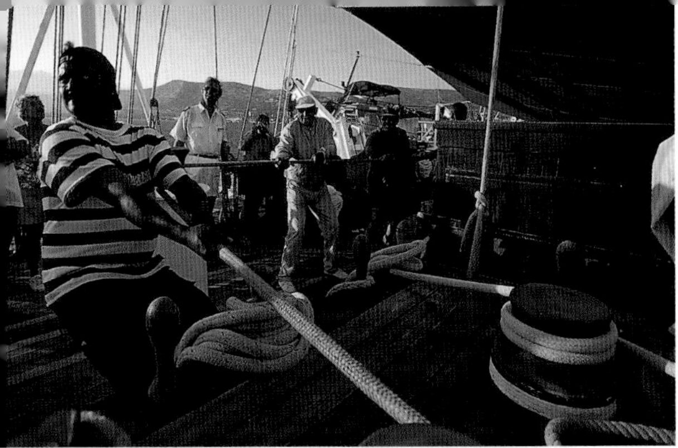

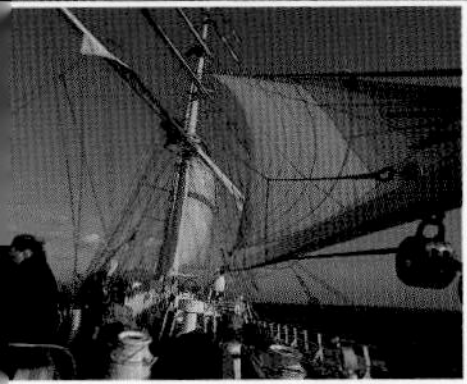

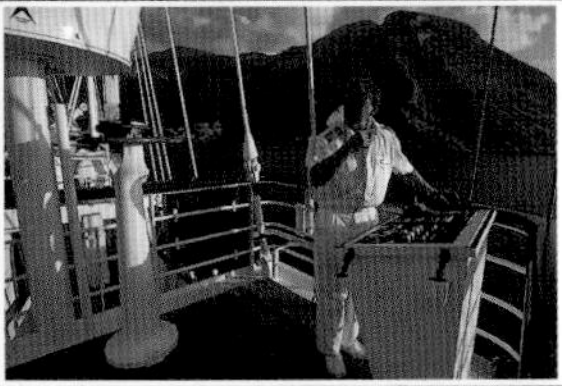

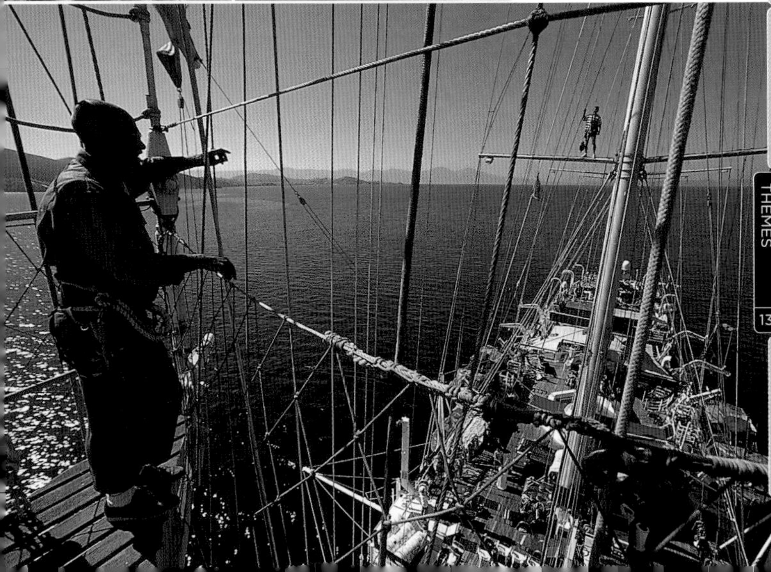

Preparation

On the road

Appreciating Light

Subjects

THEMES

137

Reference

Street life

Towns and cities offer different kinds of photo opportunities—something of the landscape in overall views, and also a wonderful setting for people in all kinds of activity. Usually, the best way to deal with street life is to shoot unobserved, and there are a number of ways of doing this. The most direct is simply to shoot very quickly, quietly, and without fuss. This is easily enough said, and some great reportage photographers like Henri Cartier-Bresson have made this approach their hallmark, but it needs astute observation and fast reactions.

Try to anticipate what people will do next in any kind of situation—how they will react or look—because this will give you the edge in capturing the expression or movement. When you see the moment that you think is right, shoot without hesitating. Many people with a camera pause out of uncertainty before pressing the shutter, and lose the chance. You have nothing to lose by shooting.

For this kind of photography, particularly in the street or other public place, like a market, a standard (efl 50mm) or wide-angle focal length is probably the most useful. A shorter focal length allows you to shoot from fairly close, which is helpful if there are a lot of passersby who might otherwise get in the way. The difficulty is that people can also see you, which may make it impossible to get a second shot that looks natural. One technique that can help is to use a wide-angle lens but compose the view so that the person you are photographing is off-center—in this way the camera appears not to be pointed directly at them.

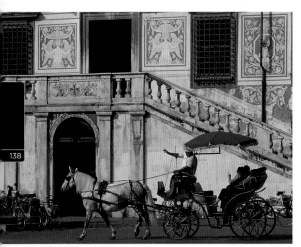

HORSE AND CARRIAGE
Tourists passing in front of the Palazzo dei Cavalieri in Pisa, northern Italy.

138

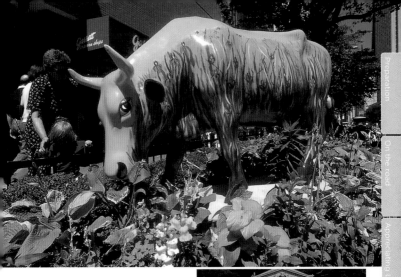

Preparation

On the road

Appreciating Light

Subjects

THEMES

139

Reference

CHICAGO COW
One of more than 300 painted fiberglass lifesize cows
placed around the city's downtown loop. The "Cows on
Parade" project was a huge publicity success for Chicago.

OLD NICE
The Cours Saleya, combining fin-de-siecle architecture
and market, typifies this old French Mediterranean port.

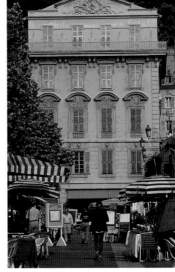

You can also make good use of long focal
lengths. A telephoto lens lets you stand at a
distance, and there is every chance that you
will not be noticed if the scene is busy—and
so can go on shooting naturally. A medium
telephoto, such as the equivalent of 180mm
for 35mm, is particularly good for "across-the-
street" shots. Longer telephotos are more
difficult to use because they are heavier, need
faster shutter speeds to avoid camera shake,
and draw attention. One technique is to sit
quietly somewhere, and shoot from there.
With all telephotos, there is a chance of
passersby and vehicles crossing in front of
the camera, so be prepared to shoot more
frames than usual.

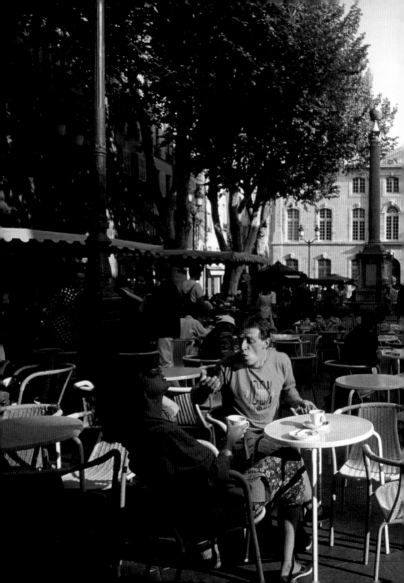

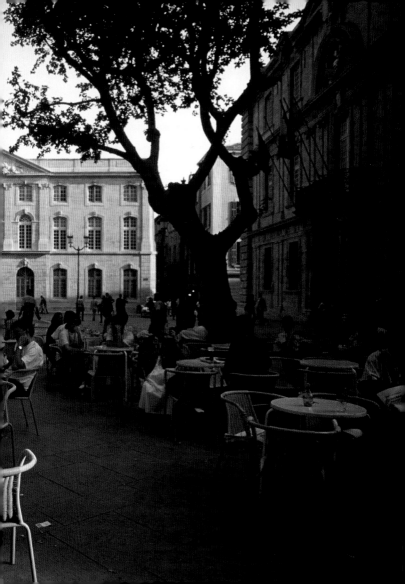

Overviews

Cityscapes, and urban landscapes in general, often cry out for an establishing shot that makes some sense of the jumble and detail of buildings and streets. Viewpoint is the first thing to consider and tends to be more of a problem than in a natural landscape. You don't have unrestricted access, and the layout of buildings always narrows the choices of clear views. Cities surrounded by hills or built on hills, such as San Francisco or Athens, have many good viewpoints, but they are the exception.

Some of the most effective shots are those taken at a distance and at some height with a telephoto lens. Try the following:

○ The top of any prominent tall building. Tall apartment buildings sometimes have open access; some public buildings may have purpose-built viewing galleries, but for offices and official buildings you would need advance permission.

○ Any high ground, such as a hillside.

○ The opposite side of a stretch of open ground or water, such as in a park, or on the other bank of a river.

Anticipate the lighting conditions that will give the effect you want. As with landscapes, a low sun in the early morning or late afternoon is usually more attractive than a high sun. Midday sunlight usually gives more contrast in a city than in an open landscape, as tall buildings cast large, strong shadows. Sunrise and sunset can be as effective as anywhere else. Cities also look good after dark, especially at dusk when there is still enough natural light to show the shapes of buildings.

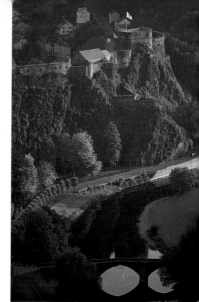

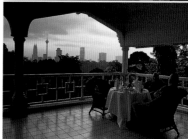

WATCHTOWER
A watchtower built on a hill overlooking the town and castle of Bouillon in the Belgian Ardennes is locally well-known, and quite easy to find from local tourist literature.

KUALA LUMPUR
The skyline of Malaysia's capital, including the Petronas Towers (for a time the world's tallest building), becomes worthwhile as an image only through being framed here by the verandah of an old hotel.

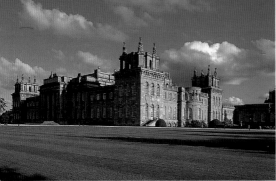

BLENHEIM
No elevated view of this famous English stately home, but a clear shot from across a huge lawn, taken with a shift lens racked up to make more of the sky.

ANGKOR WAT
An isolated hill, Bakheng, less than a mile from the temple of Angkor Wat, gives a classic view—indeed the only overview possible without an aircraft.

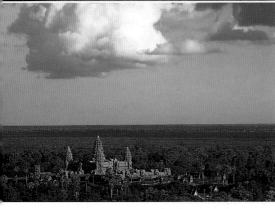

The city at night

For a nighttime shot, cities are more brightly lit after sunset, and more so in winter than summer, when offices are still full. Different types of light—street lighting, neon displays, and public building spotlights—are switched on at different times. Check the scene the evening before to guarantee the timing for the brightest array of lights.

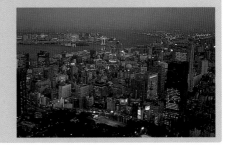

Preparation

On the road

Appreciating Light

Subjects

THEMES

143

Reference

Markets

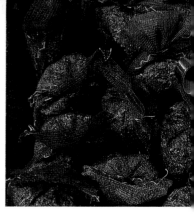

All destinations have their share of life, art, and nature; the full range of subjects for the camera, but a few stand out for their special relevance to the traveler. Markets are among these because of their variety, liveliness, and for offering an instant window into local culture. A common situation on arrival at a new destination is that of unfamiliarity. The guidebook sights apart, where do you find a concentration of people in a photographable situation? Markets are the reliable constant the world over. They are where people congregate to buy, sell, exchange, gossip, and they make an ideal entry point for photographing the community. If nothing else, an hour or two at the market is a kind of photographic exercise, a way of limbering up and brushing up your shooting skills if they're a bit rusty.

CLOSE-UP
The produce for sale is itself a potential subject for detail shots –here sachets of lavender in a Mediterranean French town, Moustiers-Ste-Marie.

MERCATO CENTRALE
Florence's best-known food market is the Mercato Centrale, housed in a cast-iron hall dating back to 1874.

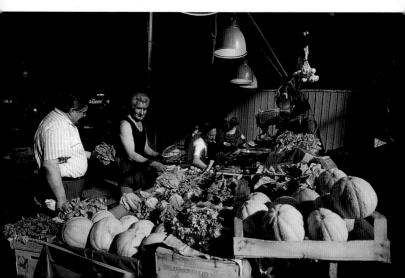

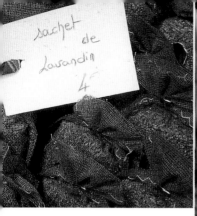

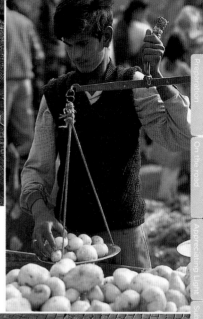

INDIA
Most Indian food markets are open-air. In a crowded street in Gwalior, a vendor weighs potatoes on a handheld scale.

ELEVATION
The Grand Place in the heart of Brussels, arguably Europe's most beautiful city square, hosts a flower market during the day. I asked permission to climb to a balcony of the Hotel de Ville for a more graphic view looking down.

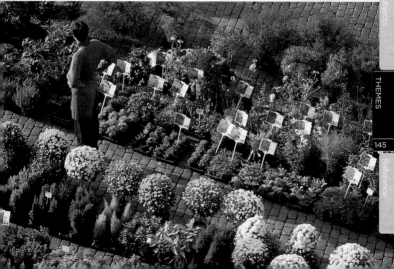

Preparation

On the road

Appreciating Light

Subjects

THEMES

145

Reference

Worship

Another reliable site where people congregate is—in most parts of the world—the local place of worship, whether a church, mosque, temple, or shrine. Like the market, there is usually a particular day and time for worship; unlike the market the activity is more serious and intense, and calls for more sensitivity on the part of the photographer—always make sure that you know in advance what you can and cannot do. There is always someone to ask.

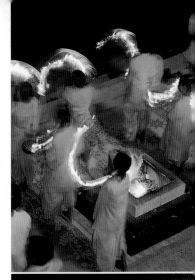

RISHIKESH: HINDU
The evening Maha Aarti (great prayer ceremony) on the banks of the Ganges at Rishikesh, a notably sacred site where the river leaves the Himalayas.

NORTHERN THAILAND: BUDDHIST
The year's principal festival at an important old temple in northern Thailand, Wat Prathat Lampang Luang, takes place on the day of the November full moon, so it made sense to shoot at the time and place where this would be visible.

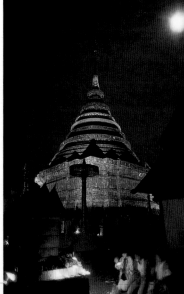

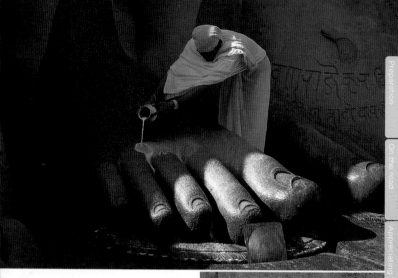

GOMETASHVERA: JAIN
A major pilgrimage site for Jain worshippers is the 56ft (17m) statue of Gomateshvara at Sravanabelagola, in India. The huge feet, over which milk is poured during a ceremony, convey the scale even more effectively than the entire statue.

WAILING WALL: JEWISH
Praying at the Wailing Wall, also known as the Western Wall, in the Old City of Jerusalem, has been a Jewish custom for centuries.

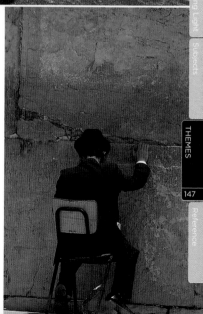

Preparation

On the road

Appreciating Light

Subjects

THEMES

147

Reference

People

Undeniably, the theme with the greatest variety and complexity that presents itself before the camera when traveling abroad is "people." There are various styles of images of people—posed portraits, reportage, people at work, people at play, and so on. All have their merits, but here we're going to explore the candid, intimate photograph—when the subject or subjects (one or two usually create the most poignant images) are entirely oblivious to the camera and the photographer.

Images such as these are usually the most successful at capturing people in quiet, reflective contemplation or deep in conversation, and their lies in their ability to provide the viewer with an entirely natural, geniune perspective of people, which draws them into the picture.

To capture such personal, intimate moments you need to be outside the subject's field of vision, yet be close enough to capture expressions. To do this you'll need a telephoto lens in the 200–400mm range. Consider the physical surroundings in which the subjects are located—more often than not, including elements of this will add context to the moment and reinforce the intimacy, whether it's someone sitting still while surrounded by a bustling crowd, or a couple holding hands while seated next to a river.

It goes without saying, you should be very sensitive to your surroundings when taking photographs of people in a public space. While officially it may not be illegal, people may take offense if they see a long telephoto lens pointing at them. Use your judgement and be as inconspicuous as possible. Also remember that if you are intending to submit such images to stock agencies, and you don't have a model release

form signed by the subjects (difficult under most circumstances), such images will be advertised as "Not released." To a certain extent this will restrict their usage, so making them less valuable.

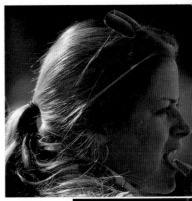

REFLECTION
A moment of quiet reflection for this young woman. The use of a telephoto lens has helped to blur the background making her profile easier to read.

A PRIVATE JOKE
Two men on an Athens' street share a moment of restrained humor.

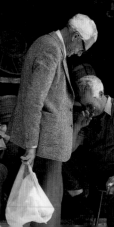

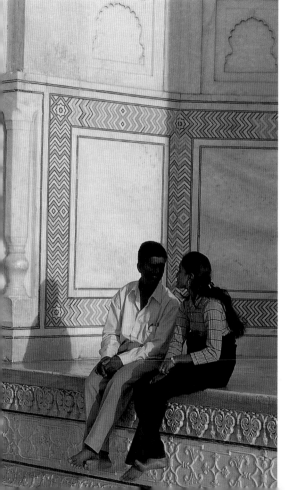

Preparation

On the road

Appreciating Light

Subjects

THEMES

149

Reference

TAJ MAHAL

An Indian couple in an alcove of the Taj Mahal (hence the bare feet, as all visitors must remove their shoes), share an intimate moment. Their almost identical body postures reveals that they are much more interested in one another than in the world-famous monument, built appropriately as a token of love.

Monuments and museums

Archeological sites call for many of the same camera techniques as regular buildings, but there are some other things to consider. Some of the more remote, or extensive, sites offer possibilities for very evocative photography. The ruins of Chichen Itza, shown here, are perfect examples of this kind of monument. On a smaller scale, there are similarly atmospheric sites everywhere in the world; only the most accessible and famous, such as Stonehenge, the Pyramids, and the Parthenon, are under so much pressure from tourism that photography is restricted.

Nevertheless, access is usually the first consideration if you are planning to photograph an archeological site. There are nearly always some kinds of restriction placed on entry to protect delicate monuments. Check these carefully before going, as well as opening and closing times, if any. You may want to shoot at sunrise or sunset, but not all monuments are open to the public at these times. In addition, check to find out if there are extra fees for photography—this varies from place to place, but in general you are more likely to be charged if you appear to be a professional photographer; also tripods may be banned. Light-sensitive artifacts, such as polychrome murals, may be off-limits for photography.

Ancient monuments more than most other buildings benefit from not having people in view, but with a large monument this is rare. The best opportunities are nearly always as soon as the site opens. Otherwise it is usually a matter of waiting for moments when other visitors are out of sight. For atmospheric shots, treat the site as you would a landscape, and try to plan the photography for interesting light—at the ends of the day,

or possibly with storm clouds. Also look for wide-angle views that take in close details such as a fragment of sculpture, as well as the distance. In addition to these basic scenic shots, consider the more documentary shots, such as a record of a bas-relief and other

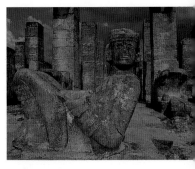

CHICHEN ITZA
The statue of Chacmool, an Aztec god, in its typical but unusual posture. Statues are now rarely found in situ because of the danger of theft, making situations like this valuable for archeological photography.

carvings. Here again, the lighting is important: raking light across the surface is usually the clearest for carvings in low relief.

Most museums do not allow casual photography. The procedures for shooting involve written permission, increasingly difficult to obtain, payment (often high), and restriction of use. As museums normally own the copyright in the works they exhibit, there is no way around this. The answer, if it qualifies as such, is just to try, but be prepared to give up when stopped. Open-air museums tend to be rather more relaxed.

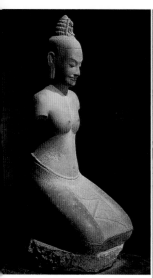

MUSÉE GUIMET
A stone Khmer statue at the museum in Paris founded with this large collection from Cambodia.

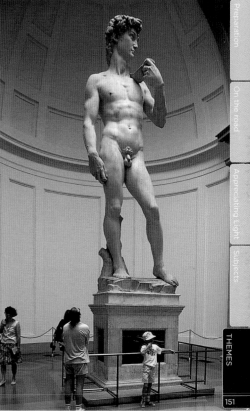

Preparation

On the road

Appreciating Light

Subjects

THEMES

151

Reference

DAVID
Sometimes, stepping back from a close view of an art object in display is worth it to show the setting and people. Michelangelo's statue David is lit by daylight at the Accademia in Florence, Italy.

Landscapes and viewpoint

At some point on every trip to a fresh area of landscape, the need sets in to find the defining shot—the single scenic image that captures the sense of place. Landscape photographers do this all the time, and don't usually limit themselves to one view that encapsulates everything. It depends on interpretation as well as opportunity, and may take a day or two of traveling around before you have an idea of what makes the scenery distinctive. Sandstone mesas and buttes punctuating the great arid distances of northern Arizona, the bocage landscape of northern France that is dense with hedgerows, the succession of alps and hillsides in parts of Switzerland—these and countless others are the themes of specific landscapes.

Catching glimpses and building up a composite view as you travel is one thing; translating this into one image is quite another. One of the odd things that happen while traveling through any landscape, whether by car, boat, or train, is that the eye and mind "see" a view that is in fact made up of many fleeting impressions. It's more akin to watching a movie, and when it stops—when the vehicle stops—the clear view of the scene usually resolves itself into a mess. Foreground obstructions in particular, suddenly appear, and often there is a frustrating lack of what the photographer has formed in his or her mind as the perfect view.

And here lies the problem—but also the solution. Expecting a certain kind of image without obstruction courts disappointment, even while it can also spur you on to making more effort. Lookovers are not the only camera positions, but they are the easiest to visualize. Viewpoint certainly makes or breaks a scenic shot, but it is often more rewarding to think through the essence of the landscape. If a forest is too dense to allow an overall view, try to work with the denseness. Deserts, steppes, and plains are often unremittingly flat, but rather than look for a way out of this by finding an elevated viewpoint, why not stress the plain, simple horizontality with a dead-on, minimalist image?

EMPTINESS
Rather than search for occasional strong features like an outcrop, I wanted here to convey the sense of emptiness in the northern Sudan desert. My only concession was a small shrub to emphasize the sense of loneliness.

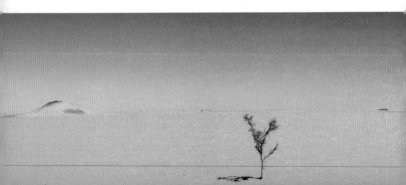

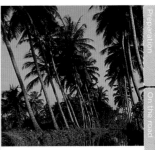

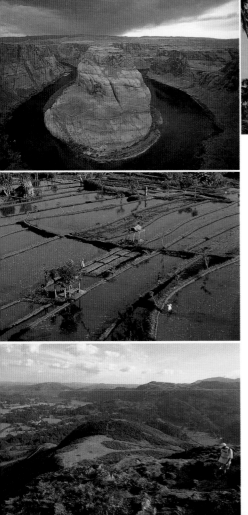

Preparation

On the road

Appreciating Light

Subjects

THEMES

153

Reference

HORSEHOE

A well-known view of the Colorado River near Page, Arizona, aptly named Horseshoe Bend. There is, in fact, little choice of viewpoint here, and it more or less dictates a very wide-angle lens.

KERALAN PALMS

In the local language, the name for the south Indian state of Kerala means "coconut palm," which abound. An overview from a distance would be less typical and less effective than the view from a small boat crossing one of the many small canals in the backwaters.

BALINESE RICEFIELDS

Clear light and an intense blue sky made this a shot to be sought after—with young rice just being planted, the water in the paddies would reflect the color of the sky. It took some time to find a clear overview from a little higher up the hill.

LAKE DISTRICT

This part of England's Lake District, near the town of Grasmere, is known for its rolling green hills, and these needed a moderate elevation to show them off.

Landscapes and light

If viewpoint is one key ingredient in capturing a successful landscape photograph, the other is certainly light. The quality of light varies endlessly with time of day, season, and weather. This is really all about timing, and having found the camera position that gives the essential view, you then need—or at least hope for—some special kind of daylight that will elevate the image from the documentary to the evocative. This, at any rate, is what most of us feel, even though the odds are, by definition, against us.

Above all, traveling ensures that you will never have enough time in any one place, for whatever kind of photograph. As photographers we are conditioned to want a certain specialness from a picture—something that sets it apart from others that have been taken before—and in shooting landscapes this usually comes down to the lighting. As two pairs of photographs here amply demonstrate, in the right circumstance a shaft of sunlight can transform an image. There is just so much planning that you can usefully make,

particularly when traveling on a schedule; weather report, time of day, and angle of the sun on key features. After that, it's a matter of how much time you are prepared to spend waiting for one shot, the odds of the light changing significantly in that time, and luck. The Spider Rock shot on the following page was definitely luck; the stormy sky held no good promise, and with no more than 15 minutes left before sunset, the view from this overlook would have been wasted if the sun had not broken through for less than two minutes. I was preparing to write off the afternoon's photography before this happened, but felt a duty to see it through, just in case.

Beyond all this is the matter of taste. The examples of lighting here are unashamedly picturesque, and you might prefer a more understated light. Choosing a certain viewpoint and composing the shot in a particular way means taking into account the distribution of light across the scene. Flat lighting, for example, is likely to suggest quite a different composition for one scenic location than would bright raking sunlight.

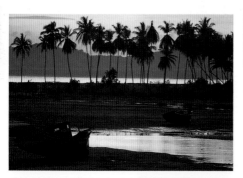

RIVERMOUTH
Deciding when to shoot is critical if you want to give yourself the best opportunity to capture your subject in complimentary lighting; here the dusk light sets off this Malaysian scene beautifully.

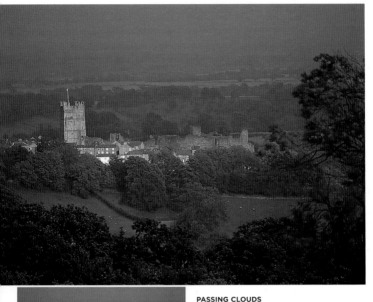

Preparation

On the road

Appreciating Light

Subjects

THEMES

155

Reference

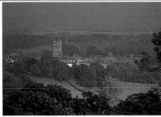

PASSING CLOUDS

The shot, of the Yorkshire market town of Richmond, was pre-determined as the job called for the first glimpse of it on a walk across England. The only variable was therefore the lighting, on a difficult day with strong winds and inconvenient clouds. The difference that a brief shaft of sun made is obvious.

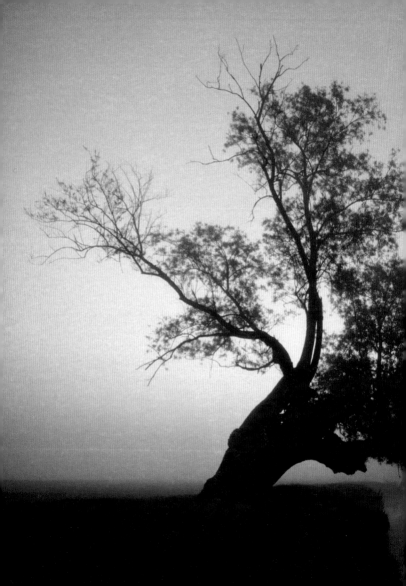

MISTY TREE
Even allowing for differences in taste, there is little doubt that this striking tree silhouette is best served by lighting that helps it to stand out from its surroundings.

Country life

Despite the high visibility and impact of cities, most of the people on the planet still lead rural lives. For the traveler this may not be immediately obvious. Most journeys to other countries begin in a major city, often the capital, because it's nearest the arrival airport. Cities are, in any case, the hubs for traveling outward, and the easiest place to arrange itineraries, buy provisions, rent cars, and organize travel documents. Nevertheless, in terms of normal life and the average human landscape, the countryside dominates. On the surface, a pattern of rice fields glistening on a lush Southeast Asian hillside may seem exotically different from the flat wheat plains dotted with grain elevators in the Midwest, but the concerns of the people who live there are essentially the same.

Life revolves around the seasons and the agricultural cycle. The busy times are planting and harvest; the communities are usually small; the weather determines the prosperity from one year to the next.

As you travel, keep this underlying continuity in mind. The specific activities you come across may be novel—repairing dry-stone walls on a Yorkshire moor, or bringing in baskets of harvested rice to a communal depot in upper Burma—and the dress and appearance of the people may add character to the pictures, but the general purpose of life is pretty much the same. Knowing this, it helps in planning your shooting to find out what crops are grown, what animals raised, and so what activities are happening at this particular season. After the harvest is in, country communities the world over have time to spare—and this is not only when things get repaired and painted, but also when festivals—even marriages—are most likely. Rural communities tend to be more conservative than those in cities, and customs more likely to be preserved.

Country life is also more distinctively regional than that of cities, where buildings, shops, and even the products for sale reflect globalization. The land and its potential can sometimes change sharply in several miles. With a sharp eye you can highlight these practical differences in your images.

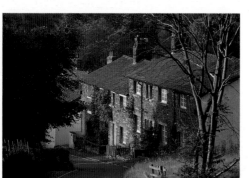

ENGLISH VILLAGE
A classic of its type, at least in terms of what people expect to see, is this view of a stone-built village in the Lake District of northern England. The viewpoint is down a steep approach road.

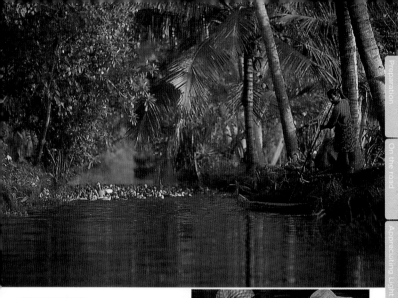

SOUTHERN INDIA
A south Indian duck farmer shoos his charges across a small canal in the Keralan backwaters in the early morning.

BURMESE RICE MARKET
Burmese women carrying sacks of rice from their own farms to the communal mill for weighing.

DRY-STONE WALL
A traditional technique in parts of the north of England, is the building of field walls without mortar, relying instead on carefully chosen stones.

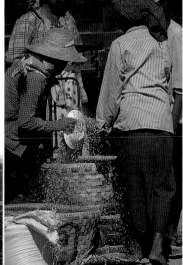

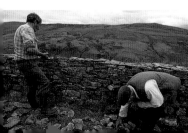

Forests

There are several kinds of forest and woodland, and the three most common of these are temperate deciduous, coniferous, and rainforest. Although many are under threat from logging and burning, they are still rich environments for nature photography (except for coniferous plantations).

Light levels tend to be low, particularly in rainforests, where the upper canopy of leaves effectively cuts off the ground from all light, and northern coniferous forests. Light levels may be too low for handheld photography and reasonable depth of field—as much as 12 *f*-stops less than the sunlight above. A tripod is always useful in these conditions. One benefit of deep forest gloom is that all the light is diffused and so contrast is low, and this helps to simplify the tangle of vegetation. At the same time, this diffusion can give a green cast to the image—this may even benefit the image, but remember that you can color-correct with the white point balance, or later on the computer.

In less dense forests, and at the edges and along riverbanks, some sunlight penetrates. This tends to give a dappled effect, which might cause contrast problems. Look for subjects (flowers or animals) that are lit by patches of sunlight and expose for these. In fact, as a general rule, the woodland edges and glades have a greater variety of animal life. Large mammals are not common, but this lack is more than compensated for by the many different small habitats, with abundant plants, insects, and fungi. Close-up photography is particularly rewarding in woodland, but this in particular usually calls for a tripod.

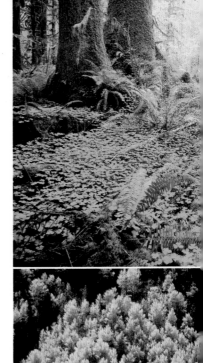

ASPENS IN FALL
Aspens turning yellow on a hillside in Colorado. The angle of the sunlight, coinciding with that of the slope, makes the most of the intensity of color.

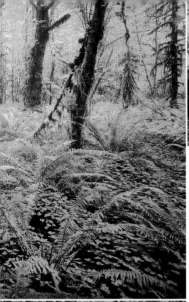

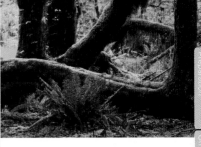

TEMPERATE RAINFOREST
Rainforest also exists, though rarely, in cooler climates, and one of the most extensive is the Hoh rainforest in Washington State on the northwestern coast. A clearing helps to open up the normally restricted view.

TROPICAL RAINFOREST
An aerial view of rapids and islands on the Upper Mazaruni River in Guyana. With dense tropical rainforest, an aerial perspective is often the only way to get a sense of the habitat in a single image

TRIPOD FOR LOW LIGHT
Forests generally have low light levels, and for static subjects such as plants, a tripod is essential. It helps if the design allows the angle of the legs to be adjusted.

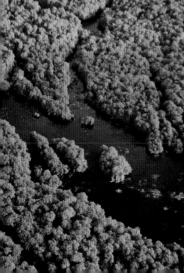

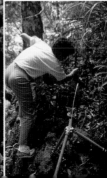

Preparation

On the road

Appreciating Light

Subjects

THEMES

161

Reference

In the detail

Closing in on the details of a scene has a number of advantages in photography. One is that it offers a refreshing change of scale to the images. Another is that it encourages graphic experiment—such as in composition, cropping, and the juxtaposition of colors. And more than this, close-ups play a key role in interpreting content—isolating a detail to focus attention. While these are universal to all kinds of shooting, travel photography stands to benefit more strongly than most. A trip of a week or two will probably result in a large number of images, and a proportion of close-ups will add a valuable change of graphic pace. Photographs of people and landscapes tend to conform to a relatively small range of compositions. There is nothing wrong with this, but close-up

shooting allows a striking freedom of imagery, even to the point of offering a visual puzzle to the audience. Detail works in travel photography because it allows the observant eye to pick out the differences in material culture and in nature. For example, the way in which the sheaves of rice have been bundled, tied, and stacked by a Balinese roadside tells much about the islanders' way of life and their own attention to detail even in the most mundane tasks. And the celebration of diversity is, after all, the underpinning of travel photography.

LAOTIAN TEMPLE
Glass mosaic set into the wall of a Buddhist chapel at the temple of Wat Xien Thong, Laos, Luang Phrabang, has a naïve charm.

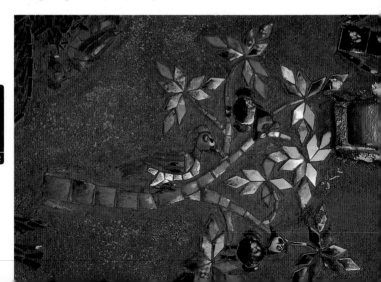

BALINESE RICE
Sheaves of freshly cut rice neatly tied and stacked by the roadside in Bali, awaiting collection.

KYOTO DOORWAY
A Japanese tradition is the noren curtain, hung in front of restaurants, shops, and teahouses. The contemporary designs, featuring symbols or calligraphy, are usually of a very high standard.

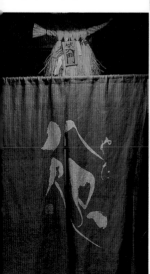

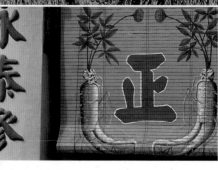

GINSENG SHOP
Shop signs are always worth looking for, particularly when they offer something out of the ordinary—here ginseng in an old-fashioned Chinese shop in Malacca.

Preparation

On the road

Appreciating Light

Subjects

THEMES

163

Reference

The ordinary

Lou Klein, the Art Director at *Time-Life* whom I quoted at the very beginning, began one briefing for a book I was about to do on a European city by saying "I want to see what the milk bottles look like." He was not being literal (although I did bring back a photograph of a bottle on a doorstep just in case). It was by way of encouraging me to shoot the ordinary, everyday things in another culture, to give an accumulated picture of daily life. By doing this it should be possible to convey something of the experience of being a part of another community—also its similarities to and differences from our own. Photographs of ordinary life and its details are potentially absorbing to anyone from another culture, because they can, at the same time, relate clearly to everyday reality anywhere, yet also highlight a way of doing things that has evolved separately.

This is all about people going about doing unexceptional things just as you would on an unremarkable day—but in an unfamiliar environment. Just as the exotic can be made familiar through photography, so the ordinary can be made into something that calls for attention.

STREET LIFE
A group of friends outside a café in a small French Provençal town.

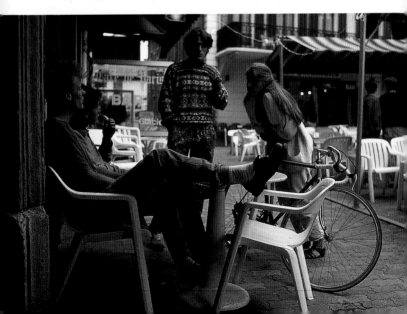

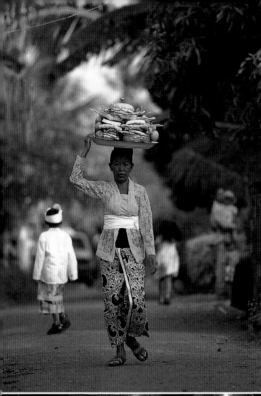

Preparation

On the road

Appreciating Light

Subjects

THEMES

165

Reference

BALINESE OFFERINGS
An island of Hindu tradition in a largely Muslim Indonesia, Bali continues to follow a largely rural way of life, despite the tourist industry. Offerings and ceremonies are the norm rather than the exception.

BRUSSELS CAFÉ
Cirio is one of Brussels' traditional café-restaurants; little changed in a century, with a regular clientele. Early weekday mornings are always quiet.

A GAME OF BOULES
On the waterfront at Cassis, a small French port near Marseilles, locals pass an afternoon playing the traditional game of boules.

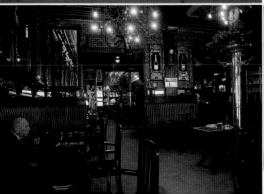

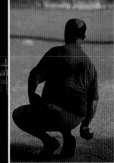

The unexpected

One of the paradoxes of travel is that it can always be relied on to deliver the unexpected. This sounds contradictory, but on the basis of experience it's true. Of course, the odds of coming across the undeniably strange corners of life are distinctly improved by traveling to, or at least wandering about in, the less obvious tourist destinations—and by doing this frequently. As far as most photographic opportunities on the road are concerned, time spent at a destination is subject to the law of diminishing creative returns. The excitement of a first sunset, then sunrise, at a Grand Canyon overlook is slightly diminished on the following day, and it doesn't take long before you exhaust the obvious. But the unpredictable, slightly weird moments that stop you in your tracks behave differently. They keep on coming the more that you travel, albeit at a much lesser frequency than the staple of scenic views, markets, and monuments. Naturally, only you are the arbiter of what counts as odd and quirky on your travels. Personally, I count the odder moments among the most satisfying from a trip.

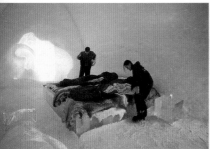

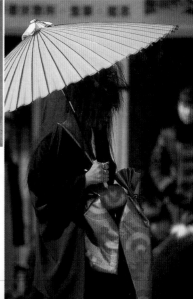

ICE HOTEL
A considered commercial enterprise certainly, but it is still remarkable that anyone would pay five-star prices to sleep on a block of ice in a hotel that melts every summer—the Ice Hotel in northern Sweden.

JAPANESE GOTHIC
Since the 1960s, Harajuku in Tokyo has been a center during weekends for the weirdest in youth fashion. It goes through changes year by year, with this odd mixture of Geisha and Goth current.

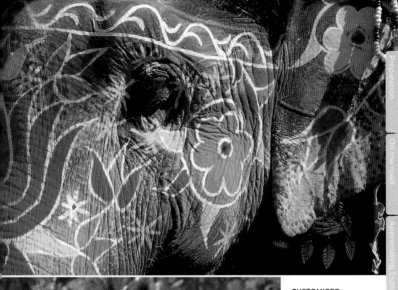

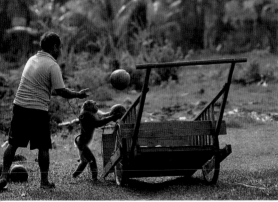

CUSTOMIZED PAINT JOB
For the Indian festival of Holi, the elephants of Jaipur, who live with their owners in the southeast quarter of the city, receive an elaborately designed coat of paint.

A HELPING HAND
This enterprising coconut plantation owner in southern Thailand saved himself labor expenses by training local macaques to do the work of climbing the palms to collect the coconuts, and then help load them.

Reworking clichés

A standard mantra of travel photography is "avoid cliché," as in "don't waste your time taking another shot of the Eiffel Tower like everyone else/or of Mount Fuji with a bullet train racing by in front." Well, yes and no. Images become clichés in a two-step process—first, the view is good, second many people take it. The word cliché comes from the French term for a photographic negative, from which identical prints can be churned out, so it's fitting that photography in particular suffers from this.

However, the problem is often that there are natural viewpoints for many scenes that just happen to work very well, if not, most photographers would choose them without prior knowledge. There is one famous view of San Francisco from a grassy hill that takes in a row of Victorian gingerbread houses in the middle distance, with downtown beyond. It works, undeniably, and has been used endlessly. Interestingly, there is just one small viewpoint from which you can see everything clearly and neatly arranged, and there is no missing the spot—the grass has been worn away by the feet of countless photographers.

There are many other examples, such as Angkor Wat from the other side of the northwest pond (the only spot that gives a reflection). The disappointment is simply that someone else got there first. As new destinations come onto the travel circuit, views that are fresh because rarely seen quickly become stale through repetition.

When faced with a popular subject, such as the Taj Mahal or Machu Picchu, the first question to ask is whether you are deliberately looking for a less-good viewpoint for the sake of being different. If you want eventually to sell the image as stock photography, that might not be sensible.

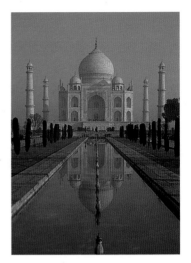

It might be better to keep the viewpoint and work some other variation, such as unusual lighting, or having someone or something different in the foreground. Indeed, foregrounds can be the savior of many views, because they make it possible to ring some changes by moving a little and perhaps by using a different focal length. The examples here are mini case histories—my on-the-spot solutions to very over-photographed locations. It is pointless to list the different compositional techniques and types of viewpoint, because such formulas are themselves clichéd. The only meaningful solution is to take time, explore, and be imaginative. And realize that any successful photographic treatment of a subject has the potential to become a cliché, simply by becoming popular.

Preparation

On the road

Appreciating Light

Subjects

THEMES

169

Reference

TAJ MAHAL

So heavily photographed is the Taj Mahal in Agra, India, that you might despair of finding a fresh view. Indeed, there really is no angle that has not been used before, but the head-on symmetrical shot down the length of the reflecting pools is certainly the cliché. More interesting graphically is the view from one side and farther back, through an arch. Not surprisingly, however, of these two images it is the cliché that sells best as stock photography.

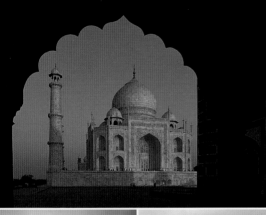

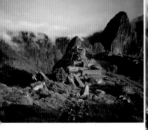

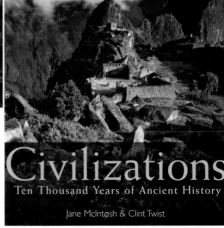

MACHU PICCHU

This ancient Inca site in the Peruvian Andes is another location with one obvious viewpoint, endlessly reproduced. It does, admittedly strike any first-time visitor as impressive, and there is no point in not trying your own version. Nevertheless, I also wanted a slightly more original view, and found it on the path down from the first position. Fortunately, one publisher also wanted a different view for a book jacket; this was the one chosen.

Civilizations
Ten Thousand Years of Ancient History

Jane McIntosh & Clint Twist

REFERENCE

Having covered equipment needs and preparation,
and discussed lighting and how to make the most of
subjects and themes, all that remains to complete this
comprehensive review of traveling with a digital camera,
is the perhaps slightly more mundane yet practical
information that will help you on your travels.

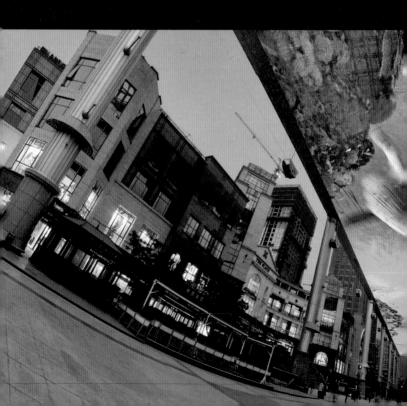

Discussed here are the different types of power sources available to you as you move around the world, image storage suggestions, security arrangements, how to negotiate customs, common legal restrictions you should be aware of, and some valuable Internet sources.

SHOPPING MALL, BEIJING
Asia's largest LCD screen, installed as a ceiling the length of a city block over a Beijing shopping mall.

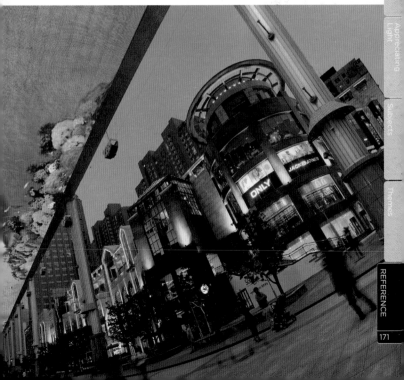

Preparation

On the road

Appreciating Light

Subjects

Themes

REFERENCE

171

Power

Not only are digital cameras totally dependent on batteries, they consume power at a high level, considerably more than conventional film cameras. Battery management is important, never more so than when traveling and far from reliable sources. There are a number of issues, but all are to do with ensuring you have enough power to shoot from day to day.

Depending on the model, digital cameras have either custom batteries or accept AA size. In the case of the former, you have no choice but to buy that manufacturer's design, and the custom charger. The number of spare batteries that you will need depends on how much you intend to shoot and the frequency with which you can recharge. Usually, on the road, it should be possible to recharge each evening. Check the specifications for battery life but do not take the manufacturer's claims at face value; test it for yourself.

AA-compatible cameras offer much more choice because of different battery types and manufacturers, though on the whole battery life is likely to be less than custom batteries (usually Li-Ion). High-capacity rechargeable batteries are the ideal, but in an emergency you can usually find AA alkalines to keep you going. There is a wide choice of chargers from independent manufacturers. It is important, however, to check the manual for types of battery that are NOT recommended. Lithium AAs emit heat and may not be suitable for all makes of camera.

Wherever there is a convenient power supply, it may be better to use an AC adaptor, usually available separately. It will also save batteries. Whichever AC device you carry with you, charger and/or adaptor, you must be prepared for the plug/outlet types in the countries you will visit. The power tables on the following pages list these.

CAMERA BATTERY
Some cameras take standard cells, many, however, take specific branded ones such as this Canon.

Battery rating

The power capacity of a battery is measured in Milliamp-hours (mAh). This indicates the battery's overall charge storage capacity, and the higher the mAh, the longer the performance. Higher capacity batteries are more expensive, but valuable for digital cameras, which have a high drain. A rating of around 1,800mAh is considered high.

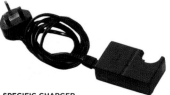

SPECIFIC CHARGER
This is the unique Canon charger for the battery shown at the top of the page. It's vital to bring your battery charger, and any spare batteries, on a long trip.

INVERTER
Relatively expensive, an inverter like the model shown left can be a useful backup when you need AC power. It converts from DC, and fits the near universal cigarette lighter socket in a vehicle. Output on this model is to the standard figure-eight socket.

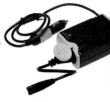

Plug adaptors

The most convenient solution to different plug/outlet types around the world is an adaptor, and this is essential for a charger or any other device that has a sealed casing. Hot-wiring (attaching bare wires from a local plug with insulating tape to the prongs of the charger or adaptor is not recommended because of the dangers of electrocution).

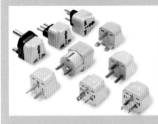

Label the AC adaptors

If you are carrying more than one device, such as a laptop or stand-alone storage as well as the camera, you are likely to have similar-looking AC adaptors. To avoid confusion, and possible damage to circuitry, label each one clearly.

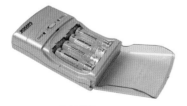

GENERAL CHARGER
If your camera uses a standard cell size, it's possible to get rechargeable batteries too. These rarely last as long as Alkaline cells though, so pack spares.

Recharging strategies

Follow the camera manual, but also bear in mind the following:
- With NiCd and even NiMH, try not to recharge before the battery is fully discharged. With Li-Ion batteries, however, shallow discharge actually increases the cycle life (a cycle is a full charge followed by a full discharge).
- Do not overcharge.
- Smart chargers may be able to do the following: discharge the battery prior to recharging, replenish charging, and switch off once a full charge has been achieved.

Battery comparisons

Alkaline. Widely available, not rechargeable, moderate capacity, keeps charge when not used.
- Nickel-Cadmium (NiCd). The least expensive type of rechargeable battery, gradually loses charge if not used. Suffers from "memory effect" in that if they are recharged before being fully discharged they "learn" to have a smaller capacity. Smart chargers can solve this problem.
- Nickel-Metal Hydride (NiMH). More expensive and higher output than NiCd. Also gradually lose power when not used, but do not suffer from "memory effect."
- Lithium (Li). Not rechargeable, light, powerful, long life, expensive.
- Lithium-Ion (Li-Ion). Rechargeable, but like Lithium are light and powerful.

Power tables

Voltages generally divided between the range 110-120v and 220-240v, with minor variations, although a few countries have both. Cycles are in Hertz (Hz), usually either 50 or 60. There are four major plug-and-socket types, with variations within each, particularly in the European group. Note that some countries have more than one plug type. Chargers and adaptors are dual-voltage, but other pieces of electronic equipment not necessarily.

AMERICAN

Am

Am

BRITISH

Br(M)

Br(G)

Br(D)

EUROPEAN

Eu(J)

Eu(K)

Eu(C)

Eu(L)

Eu(F)

Eu(E)

AUSTRALASIAN

Au

Au

Country by country

Country	Plug type(s)	Voltage	Hz	Modem adaptor
Afghanistan	Eu(C), Eu(F)	220	50	TPR
Antigua	Am	240	50	TUK, RJ11
Argentina	Eu(C), Au	220	50	TAR, RJ11
Australia	Au	230	50	TAS, RJ11
Austria	Eu(C), Eu(F)	230	50	TAU
Belgium	Eu(E)	230	50	TBG, RJ11
Bhutan	Br(D), Eu(E), Eu(F)	220	50	TFR, RJ11
Bolivia	Am, Eu(C)	110, 220	50	RJ11
Brazil	Am, Eu(C)	110, 127, 220	60	TBZ, TFR, RJ11
Burma (Myanmar)	Br(D), Br(G), Eu(C), Eu(F)	230	50	RJ11
Cambodia	Am, Br(G), Eu(C)	120, 220	50	RJ11
Canada	Am	120	60	RJ11
Chile	Eu(C), Eu(L)	220	50	RJ11
China	Am, Au, Br(G)	220	50	RJ11
Colombia	Am	110-120	60	RJ11
Congo	Br(D), Eu(C)	230	50	TFR
Costa Rica	Am	120	60	RJ11
Cuba	A, Eu(C), Eu(L)	110	60	TPR, RJ11
Denmark	Eu(C), Eu(K)	220	50	TDM, TSC
Egypt	Eu(C)	220	50	TFR, TTK, RJ11
Finland	Eu(C), Eu(F)	230	50	TFN, TSC
France	Eu(E)	230	50	TFR
Germany	Eu(C), Eu(F)	230	50	TGM, RJ11
Ghana	Br(D), Br(G)	230	50	RJ11
Greece	Br(D), Eu(C), Eu(E), Eu(F)	220	50	TGC, RJ11
Guatemala	Am, Au, Br(G)	120	60	RJ11
Haiti	Am	110	60	RJ11
Hong Kong	Br(D), Br(G)	220	50	TUK, RJ11

Hungary	Eu(C), Eu(F)	230	50	RJ11
Iceland	Eu(C), Eu(F)	220	50	TUK
India	Br(D), Br(M), Eu(C)	230	50	TUK
Indonesia	Br(G), Eu(C), Eu(F)	127, 220	50	RJ11
Iran	Eu(C)	230	50	TTK, RJ11
Ireland	Br(G)	230	50	TUK, RJ11
Israel	Own unique standard + Eu(C)	230	50	TUK
Italy	Eu(F), Eu(L)	230	50	TIY
Jamaica	Am	110	50	RJ11
Japan	Am	100	50, 60	TJP, RJ11
Jordan	Am, Br(D), Br(G), Eu(C), Eu(F), Eu(J)	230	50	TJR, RJ11
Kenya	Br(G)	240	50	TUK, RJ11
Korea (South)	Eu(C), Eu(F)	100, 220	50, 60	RJ11
Laos	Eu(thin)	220	50	RJ11
Luxembourg	Eu(C), Eu(F)	220	50	TGM
Malawi	Br(G)	230	50	TDM, TUK, RJ11
Malaysia	Br(G)	240	50	TUK, RJ11
Malta	Br(G)	240	50	TUK
Mexico	Am	127	60	RJ11
Mongolia	Eu(C), Eu(E)	220	50	TPR
Namibia	Br(D), Br(M)	220	50	TSA
Nepal	Br(D), Br(M), Eu(C)	220	50	RJ11
Netherlands	Eu(C), Eu(F)	230	50	TNH
New Zealand	Au	230	50	TUK, RJ11
Nigeria	Br(D), Br(G)	240	50	TUK
Norway	Eu(C), Eu(F)	220	50	TFN, TSC
Pakistan	Br(D), Eu(C)	230	50	RJ11
Panama	Am	120	60	RJ11
Peru	Am, Eu(C)	220	60	RJ11
Philippines	Am, Eu(C)	115, 220	60	RJ11
Poland	Eu(C), Eu(E)	220	50	TPR
Portugal	Eu(C), Eu(F)	220	50	TDM, RJ11
Romania	Eu(C), Eu(F)	230	50	RJ11
Russian Federation	Eu(C), Eu(F)	220	50	TPR
Saudi Arabia	Am, Br(G), Eu(F)	127/220	60	TAE, TFR, TUK
Senegal	Br(D), Eu(C), Eu(E), Eu(K)	230	50	TFR, TSA
Seychelles	Br(G)	240	50	RJ11
Singapore	Br(M), Br(G), Eu(C)	230	50	TUK, RJ11
South Africa	Br(G)	230	50	TSA
Spain	Eu(C), Eu(F)	230	50	RJ11
Sri Lanka	Br(D), Br(M)	230	50	TUK, RJ11
Sudan	Br(D), Eu(C)	230	50	TIY
Swaziland	Br(M)	230	50	TUK
Sweden	Eu(C), Eu(F)	220	50	TSC, TSD, RJ11
Switzerland	Eu(J)	230	50	TSZ
Taiwan	Am	110	60	RJ11
Tanzania	Br(D), Br(G)	230	50	TUK
Thailand	Am, Eu(C)	220	50	RJ11
Turkey	Eu(C), Eu(F)	230	50	TTK, RJ11
Uganda	Br(G)	240	50	RJ11
United Arab Emirates	Br(D), Br(G), Eu(C)	220	50	TAE, RJ11
United Kingdom	Br(G)	240	50	TUK
United States	Am	120	60	RJ11
Venezuela	Am	120	60	RJ11
Vietnam	Am, Br(G)	120, 220	50	RJ11

Preparation

On the road

Appreciating Light

Subjects

Themes

REFERENCE

175

Image storage

Digital photography has dynamically altered the logistics of shooting, and at no time is this more obvious and important than when traveling. No longer do you have to estimate the quantity of film you will need, or plan to replenish stock at dealers along the way. But you do have to plan for storing the images in digital media; more than that, you need to have a sensibly worked out "production flow" of image transfers that will keep pace with the way you shoot on a trip.

The numbers are easy to calculate, and start with the file size of one of your typical images. This depends not only on your camera's resolution but also on what use you want to make of it—in other words, which of the choices of image quality you go for. Most professionals and keen amateurs will use the maximum. Memory cards of whatever capacity are only temporary storage, and you will need to transfer the images from them at regular intervals. For example, a 128MB memory card will take about 100 images shot at normal compression on a 5-megapixel camera, but only about 15 in Raw format. High-capacity cards do exist, such as SanDisk's 32GB compact flash card. However, these are expensive, and many people feel uncomfortable having so many irreplaceable images all stored on one card. You may feel happier buying a number of smaller capacity cards, even though it means changing the card more frequently.

The most efficient strategy for long-term shooting (highly relevant to traveling) is to have sufficient memory cards to continue shooting until you can discharge them onto a larger hard drive. The quantities depend on your way of shooting and on the kind of subjects that you expect to come across

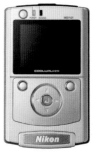
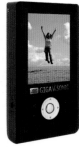

JOBO GIGA VU SONIC
One of many devices now appearing, the GIGA Vu includes a large hard disk, allowing you to copy images from a memory card, store them, and view them on screen.

CARD READER
A card reader will plug into your computer and allow you to transfer image files directly from the memory card, without the need for connecting the camera.

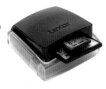

Keeping CDs safe

A padded case for carrying a number of CDs —say 10 or 20—is a useful space saver, and can be bought at most music stores.

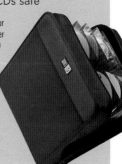

on a trip—parades and special events, for instance, tend to consume images faster.

This shines the spotlight clearly on portable long-term storage. The most immediately obvious answer, though not necessarily the best, is to carry a laptop and download images onto its hard drive. This is perfectly sound, as long as you don't mind taking a computer on the trip. Some laptops are indeed very small and light, but they still need the same care and attention as all computers.

A device that is made specifically for traveling digital photographers is the stand-alone portable storage unit that features a small, typically 2½in (6.3cm), hard drive and a port that accepts memory cards directly. There are several models available, with capacities up to 250GB, that can be AC- or battery-powered. These PDA-sized devices, which weigh just a few ounces, are convenient enough to consider carrying in a shoulder bag as you shoot. Many also feature a viewing screen that allows you to review your images.

In digitally developed countries, like Japan, many film-processing labs and camera dealers offer inexpensive copying from memory cards onto CD-ROMs. If you check in advance that this service is available at your destination, it saves time and effort and removes the need to carry your own storage media. Even in less sophisticated places, if you have a card reader you could look for an Internet café or computer center, or even the business center of a hotel, that would be willing to download your images and then burn them onto a CD-ROM.

LAPTOP CARD READER
Like the external card reader shown opposite, this is simply an adaptor for laptop computers allowing you to copy files from a memory card as if it were a disk drive.

MEMORY CARDS
Similar technology, but different shapes. Clockwise: Memory Stick, MMC, Secure Digital, Compact Flash, and the now obsolete Smart Media.

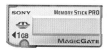

Preparation

On the road

Appreciating Light

Subjects

Themes

REFERENCE

177

Negotiating customs

There are two different considerations here: negotiating your own country's customs and everywhere else. If you are returning from abroad with more than the usual tourist's photographic equipment, you may be targeted in case you have bought a camera abroad and failed to declare it. This is one more reason for not traveling with obvious photographic cases. A sensible precaution is to carry photocopies of your equipment receipts as evidence that duty has been paid on them, and even a dated list of the equipment prepared before you leave—it proves nothing, but establishes that you are organized. Rates of duty vary from country to country, but if you do plan to buy equipment in, say, Tokyo, you should check before leaving home what the rate is —it may nullify the apparent price advantage.

Dealing with foreign customs is another matter, and likely to be a problem only if you have professional-looking equipment. Pragmatically, there are three kinds of customs:

○ Reasonable and law-abiding.
○ Strict and law-abiding.
○ Apparently strict but corrupt.

And of course this last group is the most difficult. Although rare, it does happen that you may be given a bit of a hard time over photographic equipment, and the motive may, perhaps obviously, be money. Always exercise extreme caution when attempting to bribe a customs official, even in the most blatantly corrupt countries. It puts you at risk of being accused of breaking the law, and so in even more trouble. If you are being met by a travel representative (and you might in any case consider this in "difficult" countries), ask to contact them and let them deal with the matter (the official will also be happier

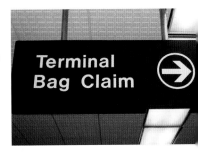

BAGGAGE RECLAIM
You won't always be this well directed as you make your way through arrivals, baggage reclaim, and customs.

dealing in his/her own language with a national than with you as a foreigner).

Digressing on corruption in general, not just at customs, the basic rule is to know exactly how it is done in that particular place, wherever it is—and the exact going rate. Techniques that work in one country do not necessarily work in another, and this is one good argument for not inserting banknotes in your passport. If you don't know how to do it, don't try.

Navigating "difficult" customs with cameras

- Do not show receipts that indicate the true value.
- Do not carry expensive equipment in original cases. This applies particularly to big lenses.
- In a corrupt country the purpose of customs harassment may be to extract money from you. Making a loud public scene is unlikely to help. Try being firm and polite, insisting that the equipment is for your personal use as a tourist to record this beautiful country.
- If this fails, try to negotiate the "import duty" down.
- In the corrupt scenario, any money you hand over is a bribe. Forget "returnable deposit". Ask for a receipt only for your own amusement.

Carnets

The ATA carnet is an international customs document that allows goods to enter foreign countries for up to one year, and although it is nearly always easier for a photographer to carry cameras as personal goods, there are occasions when it is worth the extra effort (which is considerable) to have this customs waiver, that is essentially what a carnet is. For instance, if you were doing a fashion shoot which called for cases of clothes to be taken abroad, a carnet might be the answer. The system, which allows temporary duty-free imports, was created by the World Customs Organization (WCO) and is managed by ICC's World Chambers Federation (WCF). Today, around 60 countries accept the ATA carnet.

Under the system (ATA is an acronym for "Admission Temporaire/Temporary Admission"), once you have a carnet you do not need to make a customs declaration and no duty is charged on the merchandise, provided that it is re-exported. The countries involved in the scheme accept the carnet as a guarantee that customs duties and other taxes will be paid if the goods listed in the carnet are not re-exported as stipulated within the time limit. The guarantee is made by one organization in each country, usually a chamber of commerce. In the United States, for example, the guaranteeing association is the US Council for International Business (USCIB), in France the Paris Chamber of Commerce and Industry, and in the United Kingdom the London Chamber of Commerce. The advantage is that you make customs arrangements in advance and use a single carnet to pass with a minimum of hassle through each country's customs. The carnet allows an indefinite number of trips during the 12 months that it is valid. The disadvantage is cost: between about $120 and $200 for the carnet and a returnable deposit of 40% of the value of the goods or equipment. For more information, including an up-to-date list of countries, see http://www.atacarnet.com/.

Travel security

Digital cameras and the other electronic equipment that accretes around them, such as laptops and image banks, are highly desirable. Because of the constant updates and new models, they are arguably even more desirable than film cameras used to be. From a thief's point of view you are a walking gift shop, the more so if you are traveling in parts of the world with poorer economies than your own. Add to this the inherent value of photographic and computer equipment, and it clearly makes sense to take real precautions, even if you have the equipment fully insured for the trip (as you should). According to common sense…

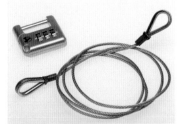

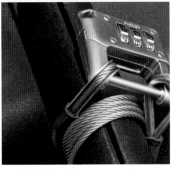

○ Never leave your camera equipment unattended anywhere.

○ Do not advertise the equipment with camera manufacturer's labels and expensive new cases, however good they may make you feel. Old and worn attracts less attention.

○ Do not leave your camera on the seat of a car with the window down, even when driving in a city.

○ If you are sitting in a well-populated place such as a restaurant or hotel lobby, never leave a shoulder bag sitting untethered or simply hanging on a chair back. Anchor it somehow, such as by slipping the strap under a chair leg.

LOCK AND STROP
Consider not only a selection of padlocks, but a strop (any line or cable fitted with hard eyes at either end). This can be wrapped around and through things to secure a variety of cases and equipment. Semiflexible stainless twisted cable like this is available made to measure from any yacht chandler.

Secure the strap

Shoulder bags have straps—use them for security whenever you put the bag down. One simple technique is to place one leg of your chair over the strap, another is to use a clip of some kind, such as a karabiner.

Local techniques

With the exception of Japan, which still has almost nonexistent street crime, most places have a community of petty criminals on the lookout for cameras and other valuables, and they develop special methods. A pillion passenger on a motorbike is one favorite, sometimes further refined into a smash-and-grab, targeting the rear windows of cars stopped in traffic.

Warning

Complacency gets you in the end. I spent 25 years traveling frequently, and to some dubious places, without having a single camera stolen—until I made the unforgivable error of locking my equipment in the trunk of a rental car one night. Never mind that it was hidden from view and that the car was securely parked in a five-star resort hotel—I'd been seen shooting the day before, and was targeted. I learned my embarrassing lesson.

TRAVEL ADVISORIES
Government agencies usually have websites on which are posted up-to-date travel advisories covering different countries and their potential hazards.

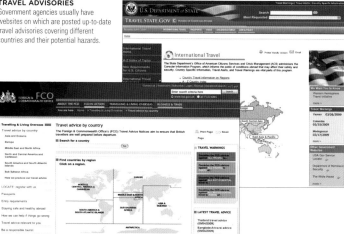

Preparation
On the road
Appreciating Light
Subjects
Themes

REFERENCE
181

Legal restrictions

By definition, these vary by country, although common sense is, as usual, a good guide. The issues that are of most importance to photographers are security, trespass, and usage rights. The first of these can really get you into trouble—all countries take military and police matters seriously. Basically, avoid taking photographs of, or even suspiciously close to, military installations such as barracks, airfields, training areas, and naval dockyards. Pay attention to signs forbidding photography.

Some countries stretch the definition of military locations and those related to national security. It is quite common for airports and docks to be prohibited subjects, and in India, for example, bridges. Nuclear power stations, dams, and even some factories may also come under the definition. In a number of countries, airports are used partly by the air force, and you should ask yourself if you really need a picture of the fighter aircraft on the other (military) side of the international airport. Probably not (and certainly not in Greece).

In civil law, the two issues that you are most likely to come up against are intrusion and unlawful use of the photographs. It is important to understand that these are separate—the first affects whether or not you can take a photograph in the first place, the second whether you can make money from it later. The law varies between countries, as does the extent to which it is upheld. The USA, for example, is notably litigious, whereas many other countries, which have similar legal protection for intrusion and privacy, are more tolerant in practice. As a rule, trespass involves entering private property without permission. You may also in some countries, be prevented from taking

Amateur vs. professional

Places that are open to the public but at the same time controlled, such as monuments, archaeological sites, theme parks, and so on, usually distinguish between amateur and professional photographers, largely on the ground of what they expect the photographer to do with the images. This makes it a gray and vague area, and in their attempts to prevent professional photography, the organizations that run such places often make arbitrary restrictions, which include:

- Use of a tripod (see page 48).
- Large or large-format cameras.
- Large lenses.
- Photographic lighting.
- Anything that gives them the suspicion that you might be professional, such as a metal case or large quantities of equipment.

ARMED FORCES
The only time you should shoot military equipment is on public display, such as at an air show or, as here in Tokyo Bay, a naval review, for which passes have been issued.

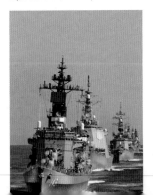

Preparation

On the road

Light

Subjects

Themes

REFERENCE

183

a photograph into private property from an adjoining public place. Nevertheless, if you have mistakenly trespassed and shot, there is hardly ever justification for a security guard to seize your camera. In such cases, the police may be your best resort.

As a photographer, you automatically own the copyright in the images, but not the subjects you have shot. This is key if you sell the photograph for purposes of trade. It does not apply if the photographs are for your own use, or if they are published editorially. The possible confusion here is that you can, of course, earn money for editorial use, but in most countries the law recognizes this as fair use. "Commercial" in this case means using a photograph to sell a product.

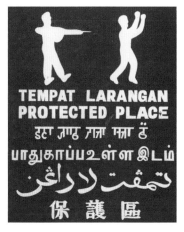

UNAMBIGUOUS
No excuse for ignoring this sign, in six languages and with consequences illustrated.

BRIDGES
Unreasonable though it may seem if you are from another country, some nations, such as India, treat bridges as essential to national security and forbid photography. If you must, be quick.

COPYRIGHTED BUILDINGS
Taliesin West, built by Frank Lloyd Wright in Arizona, is a good example of a building that, while open to the public, severely restricts photography and the use of photographs. Written permission is needed.

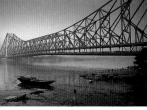

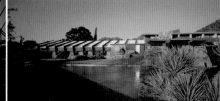

Internet resources

The Internet is now the first port of call for many photographers researching destinations. There are literally billions of webpages that you can browse to find out more about a specific location, what the weather is likely to be, and even how to get there. The more specific the information you can provide about your specific destination, the more relevant the information you'll get back.

How to access all this information? There are a number of ways, but the first step is to use a Web browser—popular browsers include Microsoft Internet Explorer, Netscape, Safari, Firefox, and Opera, although there are others. Entering the URL (the address for a webpage) in the bar at the top is the basic method of navigating to a specific website.

But with an estimated 15–30 billion webpages available on the Internet, it is more likely that you will need to search for information. There are two kinds of Web search facility, although superficially they appear similar: search engines and directories.

Search engines

These use automated programs called spiders or robots to "crawl" the Web and retrieve pages. They work by tracing hyperlinks across the Web, and this is made possible because webpages use HTML (HyperText Markup Language). HTML documents are simple, consisting of a "head" with a title and other basic descriptive data, and a body containing the document. The most popular search engines are:

Google www.google.com
All the Web www.alltheweb.com
Yahoo! www.yahoo.com
MSN Search search.msn.com
AOL Search search.aol.com

HotBot www.hotbot.com
Ask Jeeves www.askjeeves.com
Lycos www.lycos.com
Netscape Search search.netscape.com

Most search engines will return very similar results, and often choosing which search engine to use comes down to personal preference. Google is the most popular thanks to its fast and accurate search results.

Directories

These are overviews of subject categories created by people rather than by crawlers. Sites are selected and placed in a hierarchy which can then be searched. Yahoo! is the biggest and most popular of these services, yet covers less than 5% of the Web. A variation is a metapage, which is compiled by an institution such as a university or a library and offers an instant choice of hyperlinks to a particular subject. Directories include:

Yahoo! www.yahoo.com
Open Directory Project www.dmoz.org
LookSmart www.looksmart.com
... and for travelers ...
Virtual Tourist www.virtualtourist.com

Internet mapping

The interactive nature of the Internet makes it ideal for mapping services that allow you to specify the start and end points of your journey. The competition among these sites has also given rise to a number of interesting extra features, such as aerial photography, something always worth a look at before going on location.

Multi Map www.multimap.com
Mapquest www.mapquest.com
Streetmap www.streetmap.com

Google Earth

You can also download Google
Earth free from http://earth.
google.com. Google Earth is an
excellent mapping resource that
allows you to search locations,
create virtual journeys, view
animations of international
flights, and a great deal more.

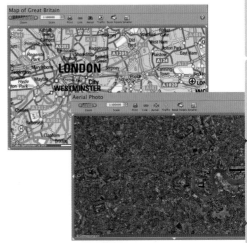

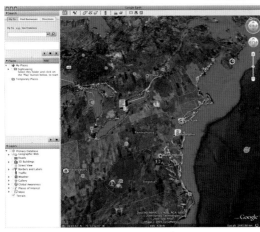

Preparation

On the road

Appreciating Light

Subjects

Themes

REFERENCE

185

Internet resources

Government advice

The Internet has many valuable sources of information for travelers. For one thing, it makes getting hold of government travel advice very straightforward. The US State Department and Great Britain's Foreign and Commonwealth Office both publish and maintain background notes on any country you might be traveling to. You should also check the front page of their "advice for travelers" sections, which will have any recently added advice.

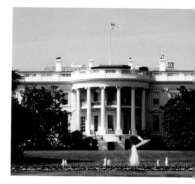

United States Department of State
travel advice *travel.state.gov*
background notes *www.state.gov/r/pa/ei/bgn/*

United Kingdom Foreign and
Commonwealth Office
www.fco.gov.uk

Health advice

Aside from concerns about personal safety, you should also be aware of health issues. Numerous organizations keep and maintain a list of health concerns, including the UN's World Health Organization's International Travel and Health guide, which is now published online and kept up to date. You may also be able to get advice from your healthcare provider.

UN World Health Organization
www.who.int/ith

US Center for Disease Control
www.cdc.gov/travel/index.htm

UK Department of Health
www.dh.gov.uk

Travel Health Online
www.tripprep.com

Equipment problems

It shouldn't happen, especially if you plan carefully and protect your equipment, but should you find yourself in need of a dealer abroad, you will be able to look up registered dealerships through your camera manufacturer's global website. If it's not possible to search a list directly, try calling the company's closest branch, since there is likely to be someone there who can help you out.

Canon *www.canon.com*
Fuji *www.fujifilm.com*
Nikon *www.nikon.com*
Olympus *www.olympus-global.com*
Pentax *www.pentax.com*
Sigma *www.sigmaphoto.com*
Sony *www.sony.com*

Preparation

On the road

Appreciating Light

Subjects

Themes

REFERENCE

Consumer photo-sharing portals

If you find yourself away from home for a long period of time, but keen to share the fruits of your photography with friends and family, you can use one of the many portals that are springing up. This wouldn't leave a great impression with a professional client, but then they will be better equipped to receive images, for example via FTP. To illustrate the simplicity of quickly sharing your images, we'll looks at the steps for Flickr's service here:

- You'll need a computer with Internet access and a way to transfer your files to it.
- Copy your image files onto your computer in the usual manner.
- Before you can upload images, you need to register to the service. This is simply a matter of filling in a brief online form.
- Once you're logged in (or registered) simply upload your images following the online instructions. You can create individual groups and sets.
- You can now email slideshows of your images or individual images to anyone with an email account. Alternatively contact them with the details of your Flickr account and they can view your images.

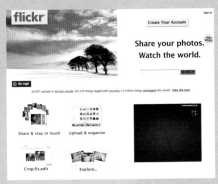

Expedition resources, news, and journals

If you're planning an adventurous trip some way from the beaten track, it might be worth reading about those who've undertaken similar expeditions in the past. This collection of sites will help you do just that.

ExplorersWeb *www.explorersweb.com*
Mountain Zone *www.mountainzone.com*
One World Journeys *www.oneworldjourneys.com*
Terraquest *www.terra-quest.com*
Web Expeditions *www.webexpeditions.net*

Glossary

ARCHIVE
The process of organizing and saving digital images (or other files) for ready retrieval and research.

BIT DEPTH
A pixel with 8 bits per color gives a 24-bit per pixel image; the more bit depth, the more colors can be digitally represented.

BYTE
A group of 8 bits; a basic unit of digital information.

CCD
(Charge-Coupled Device).
A light-sensitive imaging chip used in digital cameras. This chip sits in place of the film of a traditional camera.

CF
(Compact Flash) Card.
The most common of several types of memory cards that are used in digital cameras. The CF 'Type 2' slot can also take a small Microdrive.

CMOS
(Complementary Metal Oxide Semiconductor). A light-sensitive imaging chip used in digital cameras. It is cheaper to manufacture than the CCD chip, but the results are virtually indistinguishable.

COMPRESSION
The series of algorithms applied to a digital image to reduce its file size without sacrificing quality, at least to a point. JPEG images are compressed, whereas TIFF is a 'pure' format.

DPI
The measurement of resolution by Dots Per Inch.

FILL FLASH
The use of a camera flash in daylight to fill in shadows.

FIRMWARE
Computer instructions that are stored in a read-only memory unit rather than being implemented through software, typically refers to camera-control software.

FTP
(File Transfer Protocol). An extremely simple way of transferring large files from one computer to another.

GAMMA
The midpoint between black and white in a tonal range.

GPS
(Global Positioning Service).
A technology for identifying the exact location of a receiver using a network of Earth-orbiting satellites.

HISTOGRAM
The histogram is a graph showing the distribution of tones in an image.

ICC COLOR PROFILE
The International Color Consortium defines color profiles to help get correct color reproduction across devices.

INMARSAT
(International Maritime Satellite Network) An established and reliable network of five communications satellites in geostationary Earth orbit.

ISO
As with ASA on a film camera, a measure of light sensitivity. You can often adjust this just as you would switch films.

JPEG
The now-standard file format for digital images on the Web. JPEG, also known as JFIF, takes areas of 8 x 8 pixels and compresses the information to its lowest common value. Created by the Joint Photographic Experts Group.

MEGAPIXEL
The standard unit of measuring image size in digital cameras. One "megapixel" is one million pixels.

MOIRÉ
An interference pattern that occurs in print when dot screens are aligned at the wrong angles. The same effect can be produced by mismatched scanner-image resolutions.

NOISE
The random pattern of small unwanted spots in a digital image that are caused by stray electrical signals.

PHOTOSHOP
A powerful software program from Adobe Systems used to manipulate images. Pictures can be dramatically changed using Photoshop: colors can be altered, images sharpened, and parts of the picture removed or moved.

PHOTOSHOP ELEMENTS
A consumer version of Photoshop with fewer features, but is still very useful for manipulating images.

PHOTOSITE
The small area on the surface of a photodiode in a CCD or CMOS image sensor that captures a light level for a pixel in the image.

PIXEL
Derived from the term "Picture Element," the smallest unit of a digitized image. Each square dot that makes up a bitmapped image carries a specific tone and color value.

PPI
Pixels Per Inch. A measure of the resolution of a bitmapped image. (See also DPI and Bit depth.)

PROSUMER
A marketing term used to describe the intermediate market for camera equipment, between the consumer market and the professional market.

RAM
(Random Access Memory) The working memory of a computer, to which the CPU, or Central Processing Unit of the computer has direct access.

RAW
A file format created by most high-end (DSLR) cameras, containing all the pixel information with no compression. Each camera manufacturer has its own version of Raw. For Nikon, it is the Nikon Electron Format NEF.

RESOLUTION
The amount of detail shown in an image, whether on screen or printed. Resolution is measured in dots per inch (dpi) in print or pixels per inch (ppi) on screen.

RGB
(Red, Green, Blue). The three primary colors of light, and the system used by computer monitors to display images.

ROM
(Read Only Memory): Any memory disk or media that can only be read, not written to. ROM retains its contents without power. Most CDs, once burned with data or images, become read-only (i.e. CD-Rom).

SD
(Secure Digital) A postage-stamp-sized flash memory card that has a locking switch that can prevent accidental erasure of data once engaged.

SHUTTER LAG
The time elapsed between the moment when the shutter is depressed and when the image is captured, which can range from irritating to imperceptible.

THREEG, 3G
A new "third generation" wireless standard promising increased capacity and high-speed data applications up to two megabits.

THUMBNAIL
A miniature representation of a larger image file for onscreen viewing or printed contact sheets.

TIFF
(Tagged Image File Format). A cross-platform image file format for bitmapped images that has become a standard for high-resolution digital photographic images that are going to be printed. Some Raw formats are essentially TIFFs.

USB
(Universal Serial Bus). A standard port on most modern computers for the connection of external devices from keyboards to memory card readers.

WHITE BALANCE
A camera control used to balance exposure and color settings to correct any color cast that may not be visible to the human eye.

WIFI
From "Wireless fidelity," used generically when referring to any type of 802.11 network, whether 802.11b, 802.11a, Airport, and so on.

ZIP
A method for compressing files on a computer for storing and transmitting them at a reduced size.

Preparation

On the road

Appreciating Light

Subjects

Themes

REFERENCE

189

Index